uming Fire, Creator, Deliverer, Dwellin

s, God of All Comf [barcode] lp, Hidi

eeper, King of King My He

nd eart y Streng

er of Al d, Shiel

My Lif ega, Yah

ing Fir lling Pla

of All ding Pla

King o ead, Lig

h, My gth, Prin

, Savio d, Stron

FROM

DATE

e, The Alpha and the Omega, Yahweh, Al

, Creator, Deliverer, Dwelling Place, Ete

mfort, Healer, Help, Hiding Place, Holy (

gs, Lifter Up of My Head, Light, Lord of

y, My Song, My Strength, Prince of Peac

suming Fire, Creator, Deliverer, Dwelli

ess, God of All Comfort, Healer, Help, Hic

Keeper, King of Kings, Lifter Up of My H

and earth, My Glory, My Song, My Stren

ler of All, Savior, Shelter, Shepherd, Shie

f My Life, The Alpha and the Omega, Ya

ning Fire, Creator, Deliverer, Dwelling P

d of All Comfort, Healer, Help, Hiding Pl

, King of Kings, Lifter Up of My Head, Li

rth, My Glory, My Song, My Strength, Pr

ll, Savior, Shelter, Shepherd, Shield, Stro

ife, The Alpha and the Omega, Yahweh, A

re, Creator, Deliverer, Dwelling Place, Et

Comfort, Healer, Help, Hiding Place, Holy

ings, Lifter Up of My Head, Light, Lord c

ory, My Song, My Strength, Prince of Pe

Sacred Prayer

90 DAYS OF
DEEPER INTIMACY WITH GOD

A JOURNAL

ANN VOSKAMP

THOMAS NELSON
Since 1798

CONTENTS

Dear you—you're in the right place . . . a sacred place. Because the goal of life is not to acquire and accumulate. *The goal of life is to face the sacred face of God, who is love.* Here is a sacred space for you. Here is your sanctuary. Here, these pages are your cathedral, a hushed and holy space for your soul to intimately meet with its Maker, a place for all that is eternal, a place to commune with the tender grandeur of God.

This is a sacred space for your most significant work: The place where your soul does the work. This has become my daily way of life, a sacred rhythm and rule of life that has transformed me. And as I've shared how to live this SACRED way of praying and thinking and being and living, it's profoundly changed the lives of countless others too. A psychiatrist wrote me to note that in all of her more than four decades of working toward wholeness with countless clients, she has not found a set of personal guideposts more helpful for genuine life transformation than committing to this daily SACRED prayer and spiritual practice that ground the soul in Stillness, Attentiveness, Cruciformity, Revelation, Examine, and Doxology. Which lead the soul into deeper wholeness.

Here, in this moment, *you can begin.*

And you don't have to have it all together—you simply get to let the Father, Son, and Spirit come together around you.

You don't need perfection to step onto this holy ground—you only need honesty. Honestly: Where are you? Honestly: Where are your hopes, your dreams, your heart, your mind, your prayers? Where are you coming from? Where are you going? Honestly: What do you want—really?

This is truly your safest place—because here is where you share your truest self. To journal is to discover the architecture of your heart. No one builds a space, a dream, a cathedral without putting pen to paper. Few can solve a complex design quandary, an intricate math problem, or a circuitous, bewildering maze without reaching for the unlocking key of pen and paper. All problems beg for a piece of paper.

Your heart has its problems. And it's begging you for a sacred space and the gentle end of a pen, to pick open its lock, to finally discover the answers.

This makes a world of sense. Because this is more than a world made of atoms and physics; this is a world of story, a world made of words, by the Word. And when you put your heart into words on the page, the Word Himself works in holy ways through your words to give you a new heart.

This kind of writing is never anything less than holy. As you write words, the Word comes to meet your words, the Word comes to work in your words, the Word comes to miraculously restore and re-story you through your words and His. Here is holy ground.

The whisper of turning these pages stirs the very heart of God.

Line these pages with words, and your life can begin to align with the Word—the Word who is the singular lifeline in the whole of the universe. Order words on the page, and you bring order to your days, your life, your soul—as your life and all loves are rightly reordered.

The life you live *out* is a function of how you explore the life *within*. The more you pay attention to your interior world, the more your days will be spent meaningfully out in the world.

Journaling transforms the journey. And putting marks on paper changes the way you leave your mark on the world.

As research indicates: Accept and process what's in your mind, and you literally improve the health of your mind.[1] Journaling, organizing words on a page, is a way of actually organizing thoughts and feelings in your life. Getting thoughts and feelings down on paper gets them out of your head and frees up more space in your life. Then, when we write down the rest of our thoughts and feelings as sacred prayers to God, what we are doing is not only giving our working memory a rest from working on these problems; we are leaving them in the hands of God, trusting that He's working good through all these problems.

And studies further prove: Put words to rest on the paper, and you physically rest better.[2] Commune with God on the page, and you have a stronger immune system.[3] Ultimately: Disclosing your thoughts and feelings on a page can bring closure to painful experiences in your life.

Literally: Words heal wounds.

You are holding in these pages the possibility of a holy kind of miracle: *Shape your distress into words*, and your distress begins to heal. How? This is a sacred space that allows you to approach your pain, approach your God, instead of ignoring both.

Hudson Taylor—a short, shy man whose faithful work sharing the gospel in China in the 1800s led to the conversion of 125,000 Chinese Christians—knew a tender, heartbreaking suffering and woundedness. In one single summer, he lost not one but two of his children, and then his wife, about which he wrote:

> I feel utterly crushed, and yet "strong in the Lord and in the power of His might." Oft-times my heart is nigh to breaking . . . [but] I never knew what peace and happiness were before—so much have I enjoyed in the very sorrow . . . I could not have believed it possible that He could so have helped and comforted my poor heart.[4]

When asked how he navigated through a wilderness of heartache and disorienting loss, Taylor said he had this rhythm with a soul compass, a sacred way of living, that kept him turning back to face the face of God, who is love. This practice he called "the continuous habit of soul" kept him drinking deeply of the even deeper love of Christ.[5] It was this *continuous habit of soul* that sustained him, that kept him with God.

For me, my own *continuous habit of soul,* my own way of life that keeps me in the Way Himself, the continuous habit that sustains me, is this acronym—*SACRED*—which emerged from my study of God's people's exodus from a great power's bondage and into bonding with a great God who is the most powerful.[6] Caught between the Red Sea and the Egyptians coming at them, the people of God were not only desperately seeking a way through; what they ultimately were seeking, whether they were initially aware of it or not, was a sacred way of life to move them into intimate communion with God who is our promised land.

This daily way of prayer with pen, with this acronym SACRED, ends up parting the waters, disciplining the internal waves of worry, and making a way into the promised land of the wraparound presence of a God who holds us safe.

This SACRED way of life, an intimate prayer, a continuous habit of soul, a rule of life, a daily rhythm of journaling prompts, can literally make a way through life because it keeps one's soul in the Way Himself, as one keeps pace with God and the rhythms of the acronym:

S tillness to know God

A ttentiveness to hear God

C ruciformity to surrender to God

R evelation to see God

E xamine to return to God

D oxology to worship God

SACRED prayer with a pen—this *continuous habit of soul* that parts our waters and carries us into the intimacy of the promised land of God—simply begins with setting aside time daily.

Your healing is worth the fifteen minutes a day it takes to slide a pen across these pages. The Word is here to hear all the words about what aches and how the heart breaks, and here is a sacred space that is safe to hold your soul poured out.

And all your healing asks is for you to honestly write out your feelings, your thoughts, your story, especially the painful parts, before the witness of the Word Himself, who reads your story as a prayer of healing—and whose presence, whose witness and *with*ness in your story, brings just that: the wholeness and completeness of shalom, deep peace in Him.

Genuine prayer is a genuine conversation with our Father; put pen to paper as prayer, and lay your head, your heart, in His sure, safe, faithful hands. Prayer isn't giving God information to act upon, but God giving us intimacy to rest in. What undergirds every single prayer is the reality that we are held by our Father. These pages are truly your safest place in the world because here is where you tell your story most truly . . . *to Him.*

Ultimately, when we put words on the page, we move ourselves far enough away from our thoughts to actually see our thoughts instead of being swept up in them—and when we have enough perspective to see our thoughts, we can see a bit more of what needs to be done within us to change our stories. And, as we enter into this sacred work, we can begin to *really* see to it . . . and trust that God is going to see to it. That God is going to be doing redemptive work through it all.

To begin every day, you may turn an hourglass timer for your SACRED prayer-with-pen session, or light a candle and set a gentle alarm, or you may simply come to this spiritual practice . . . of just coming to the page. Embrace that this is hard and holy work that may feel uncomfortable in the moment, and these daily SACRED journaling prompts may touch bruised places within, as you still and attend to the heartache you've lived through and where your story and soul have been. It may feel tempting to avoid or brush past or gloss over the painful or upsetting or anxiety-ridden parts of your soul and story. But this practice of journaling isn't frivolous navel-gazing. Rather, it's about seeing whether you're tethered to things indestructible. It's about the storyline of your life following the Word Himself.

As you daily come to this SACRED space of prayer-with-pen, making this communion with God your continuous habit of soul, you can be assured that, for one, "journaling offers us better psychological and physical health,"[7] and that, far more importantly, you with your pen-as-prayer can be the scribe who came to Jesus and said, "Teacher, I will follow you wherever you go" (Matthew 8:19).

This is the WayMaker's world—and this daily soul compass that keeps turning us toward the Way Himself, who holds the whole world, will begin to tenderly make our broken hearts whole.

The daily SACRED spiritual practices of stillness, attentiveness, cruciformity, revelation, examine, and doxology can be your continuous soul habit, a way of life, a way through life, a way of staying on the way, in the way, of the Way Himself, Jesus.

Life is ultimately about distance—distance in relation to God and people—and how to daily shorten the distance and move toward intimacy. And SACRED is a way of life that erases distance, turning us throughout the day toward the face of God, who is love. SACRED keeps us drinking deeply of the love of God as our continuous soul habit, and when you let Him love you through a SACRED love, set apart for Him, your whole life can turn around.

Put one word down after the other, turned in the right direction, and you can have a whole other life—*a life that makes you whole.*

A whole and full life in the SACRED love of Christ.

Beginning

Your SACRED way, your SACRED prayer journey, begins today.

Every day is day one—and whatever you are facing today, you always, always, always get to begin again and keep beginning again.

As you begin this sacred journey into the heart of God, of moving toward deeper intimacy with Him, ask yourself: "Where is my soul, really? Where is tender, where is wounded, where is bruised, where is healing?"

What if you made a commitment to enter the chambers of His heart over the next ninety days and let Him touch the tender, fractured parts of the chambers of your own heart, to heal you in ways you've always hoped for? Right in this moment, God is looking for you, looking into your eyes, because He wants you so close you can look right into His heart for you.

"Where are you?" is God's first recorded question in all of history (Genesis 3:9), the shortest question of the entire Hebrew Bible, and it hasn't stopped echoing across the topography of time. God will always come looking for you because He wants to be with you. He asks us: *Where are you?*

In Hebrew, that question is only one word: *Ayekah*. God is speaking that one word into this moment, even right now: *Ayekah*. Where are you going with your life? Is this truly where you want to be?

When an all-knowing God asks a question—"Where are you?"—isn't He only asking so you will begin to know the answer? In this moment, God is really asking you:

"Where are you in relation to Me? Where have you gone that's taken you further away from Me? Where are you when the expectation is that you and I would always be together? Where are you, if you are not here with Me?"

God's first known question of history asks you to see where you are in relation to Him, to locate your soul nearer to Love Himself, so you can have a real and intimate relationship with Him. God's haunting, aching cry is searching for you, because He means to shorten the distance between

Him and you, His beloved. You are captivating to the point that God bound Himself to you and the cross. He wants to be with you in this sacred place. He hopes to hear your heart on these pages.

Over the next ninety days, all along the way every day, expect God to come looking for you. Expect God to want to be with you, expect God to knock at your door, expect God to rise on your horizon, expect hope and mercy and a glass of cold water—but don't expect God to come looking any way you expect. Expect mystery . . . and manna . . . and miracles . . . and a map that points the way higher up and deeper into the heart of the Way Himself.

Hear the ache of God's heartbeat for you right now: "Ayekah? *Where are you?*" Pick up a pen today to journal your heart in prayer: Where is your heart, really?

If you have a relationship with God, your greatest need isn't to figure out a way through; your greatest need is to figure out:

- Where are you in relation to God?
- Where do you find your soul, really?
- Where are all those hopes of yours taking you?
- Where are all those dreams of yours taking you?
- Where are all your plans and expectations taking you?
- Are they in the way, between you and God, or are they all making way for you to draw nearer to Him?

You know you are on the SACRED way when you don't let anything get in the way of you and the Way Himself.

The way to always begin anything is to begin to still everything.

Stillness is your strength.

In a wild, wearying world, this is the realest reality: The only way to still stay standing is to make time to stand still. This is what your soul needs to know in this moment: You don't need to strive, you don't need to strain, you simply need to still.

Because your stillness says you're trusting Him still.

This art of being still is hard. Stillness may be the most difficult to learn, and it takes time and prayerful practice. As the theologian of old, F. B. Meyer, wrote, "We must cultivate the habit of stillness in our lives, if we would detect and know God."[1] This habit, this way of life, of interior soul stillness—this will take time to learn. But we absolutely must learn the spiritual practice of stillness if we want to know God.

This matters: No stillness—no God. But know stillness—know God.

In the story of the Exodus, when the people of God are looking for a way out of a disaster, a way beyond the overwhelm of an attacking horde, and a way through the Red Sea, God Himself is all the verbs in the story of the way through the sea. God will do the moving—you must simply still.

Do you hear the Word of the Lord for you—*you*—today?

"The LORD will fight for you; you need only to be still" (Exodus 14:14 NIV).

God knew this would always be the battle, whatever waves you are battling today: Your battle is to keep still—while God does the battle. Your battle is to still—and, no matter what, to trust God still. This is the strange miracle: Stillness is always your first step through any Red Sea Road.

The fear of any storm falls away when we still long enough to be in awe of God. *In your stillness, your God moves.*

"Be still and know God" is what the psalmist beckoned in chapter 46. The literal translation of "be still" in Psalm 46 is *raphah*—which actually means to drop, to hang limp, sink down, to let go.[2] God's invitation to us to know Him is an invitation to still long enough to simply let go—let go—of all the fears and worries that have a hold on us—so He can hold us.

Right in this moment, imagine one situation you'd do anything to fight to change, one thing you wish had a wildly different story. Now, be still . . . which literally means letting your hands hang limp, letting your arms sink down. And simply let God hold you.

You can only truly let go of the thing you're holding tightly when you trust how it's completely safe in God's hands. You can only truly be still in your soul when you trust your life is better in the hands of God than yours.

Be still—why?

Be still—to know God.

Why know God? Because the greater the knowing of God, the greater the trusting in God. Trust in God—and you start to doubt having any real fears in this world.

The depth of your trust for someone is a function of the depth of your knowledge of that someone. Be still and know God—because the greater the knowing of God, the greater the trust in God. What I have realized in my journey through all kinds of heartbreak is: If I have trust issues with God, the real issue is that I don't really know God.

What would happen today if every time you felt a need to hustle, you hushed your soul and stilled?

What if you saw every need to hurry as a kind of warning light on your internal dashboard—signaling you to still?

When you take time to still, you aren't falling behind; you are letting everything else fall away, *and letting God alone be your way.*

The way of Jesus is to have a regular rhythm and spiritual practice that always begins in stillness. Jesus Himself "would withdraw to deserted places and pray" (Luke 5:16 NRSVA).

If you want to learn the art of stillness and knowing God, you have to ask your soul:

- What are you willing to withdraw from to be still and draw close to God?
- Where in your mind, in your soul, do you need to stop racing and simply be still right now?
- How do we have a way of life that takes the way of stillness— because who can afford to miss the actual way to know God?
- Can you begin by practicing stillness just two minutes every day? First thing, before your feet hit the floor, before the waves of the day hit, can you be like an Israelite and take two minutes to be still, soul-still, and gaze on God, simply trusting He will make a way through your day's waves?

Right now, wherever you are on the way, can you hush all the interior roar, close your eyes, take a deep, long breath, and quiet everything in your mind so God can calm your soul?

After you let God still the waves within, the roar of the inner storm, and the thunder of the overwhelm—simply by turning and gazing on the beauty of Him who suffers with you and who fights for you—listen right now. Can you hear it in the quiet sanctuary of your soul? *"Peace! Be still!"* (Mark 4:39 ESV).

God holds you *still.*

While the world says what gets heard is all the loudest voices, and jockeys hard to get our ear, the very Word Himself, Maker of the world, is coming to you right now through a wilderness of worries, to say, not in the roar, not in the storm (1 Kings 19:11–12) but as He comes in the lowest, stillest, quietest whisper, to beckon to you over and over again, every morning, every evening: *"Peace! Be still!"* (Mark 4:39 ESV).

Our interior stillness is evidence that our actual living address is in the spacious, non-anxious presence of God. When we embrace interior stillness with God, we surrender our outer limitations to God.

Interior stillness says we are not dependent on endless work, but on the endless provisions of Love Himself. Interior stillness is resistance against the anxious system of Pharaoh, all the systems that force us into this constant crisis to produce more and more bricks to earn our worth—and choosing instead to still and rest in the immovable foundation of our identity in Christ as His beloveds. Our God is not about building empires of productivity, but about building relationships of intimacy.

How can you set aside moments, prepare for moments, especially when the waves are rising higher, to practice returning to stillness with the One who is the King of the universe and on His throne still?

- Could you lay the Word out open on a counter—to return to and still with, to hear the quiet whisper of God throughout the day?
- Tuck a verse, a word from the Lord, in a pocket. Tape it to the back of your phone. Where else can you sit still with the Word?

What if you set one gentle reminder on your phone, to still at a set time every day, perhaps noon, to pause in prayer every day, or read a Psalm, or simply to be still, breathe deeply from a posture of trust, and know and reflect on the glory of God?

Today, in all the sacred moments on the way, if we truly want to hear from God, we get to make cathedrals in our moments. We can quiet all the noise, be still, and listen for the gentle hush of the Holy Spirit to whisper through the Word so we don't miss Him. To learn the language of the God who speaks in whispers, you must learn how to be soul-still. To hear from God, we must be still before God. Stillness is how we listen.

Your life changes when you practice a way of life that isn't afraid of the stillness—even though stillness is always its own kind of wilderness. Never, ever be afraid of any stillness, or any of your wildernesses.

Strikingly, the Hebrew word for wilderness is *midbar*, also read *m'ca-ber*, which means nothing less than "speaking." The wilderness is where the Word speaks and where the Word can be heard—and where we can be formed into people of the Word. The promised answer to our prayers may not be found in promised lands, but in the stillness of our wildernesses. Linger long here. *Every wilderness, every desert, is not where God deserts—but is where God woos with a whispered Word.*

Listen to Him speak:

> This is what the Sovereign LORD, the Holy One of
>   Israel, says:
>   "In repentance and rest is your salvation,
>   in quietness and trust is your strength"
>   (Isaiah 30:15 NIV).

Quiet the crush of everything; be still and trust.

Ask your soul:

- Why are you afraid of stillness?
- Why are you afraid of wildernesses that can hold stillness?
- What do you think might happen if you simply stilled?
- Would you struggle less if you simply stilled more?
- Are you afraid to still because a part of you thinks that if you do, it will be up to you to part the waters on your own?

You will only have as much strength as the strength you have to be still.

You will only ever have as much strength as the strength you have to enter the wilderness and find stillness. And when you have the strength to enter the wilderness that holds stillness—you will be still and know God. And knowing God is what makes you strong, is what heals you. Stillness in your wilderness is the first step on the way to soul healing and real strength. *Your every wilderness can be a place of clarifying stillness.*

Stillness is how the soul embraces God's will . . . and stillness equips us to finally let go of trying to be our own gods still.

How can you carry that stillness, the stillness of being safe with God, into your day?

This is always your invitation, to come the way of Jesus Himself, as the sacred text of Mark 1:35 reads: "While it was still very dark, [Jesus] got up and went out to a deserted place, and there he prayed" (NRSVA).

You don't have to be afraid of the stillness because in the practice of this new way of life, a way of life like Jesus, the first step of the journey requires stillness, which lets you hear, and not miss, listening to the Way Himself. As Ole Hallesby, the Norwegian theologian, wrote, "The greatest blessing connected with stillness is that we can hear eternity; we can hear the voice of the Eternal One as He speaks to our conscience."[3]

By stillness, sanity is found.

Still—and let go of what has hold of you.

By stillness, sense is made of things.

Still—and let it all fall away—so you can see the Way Himself, who is your way.

By stillness, the roar of the Enemy is stilled, and the soul can listen to the whisper of its Maker, its WayMaker.

Still—and let go of all your control. Still—and rest in how your very own kind Father is in control.

Hush all the worry and hurry. *Be still . . . and live into a tender surrender of a life of prayer, because the Lord Himself fights His way to you, fights for you in ways you don't even know you need.*

To practice stillness is to practice defiantly trusting in prayer: You can still and trust that God is still moving, working all things into good.

Wherever we simply still and slow the soul in prayer, we are whispering: *Not my will, but solely my Father's will.*

Make time to be still—in order to make it. In order to make a full life.

Still hearts still see God.

stillness to know God

How can I slow, still, and breathe in a place of trust with God today? (Psalm 46:10)
Still all the worry.... Hush all the hurry.... Breathe ... breathe deeply....
I live in the spacious, non-anxious presence of God.

_____

attentiveness to hear God

Who do I say that God is today? (Mark 8:29)

_____

_____

_____

Where am I coming from and where am I going to today? (Genesis 16:8)

_____

_____

_____

What do I want today? (John 1:38)

_____

_____

_____

cruciformity to surrender to God

What do I need to do or surrender to live cruciform today? (Luke 9:23)

_____

_____

_____

revelation to see God

How did I experience a fresh revelation from God in His Word today? (Psalm 119:105)

---

examine to return to God

What am I afraid of today? (Mark 4:40)

---

doxology to thank God

What can I thank God for today? (1 Thessalonians 5:18)

What's God inviting me to do today, to make today a day of more amazing grace?

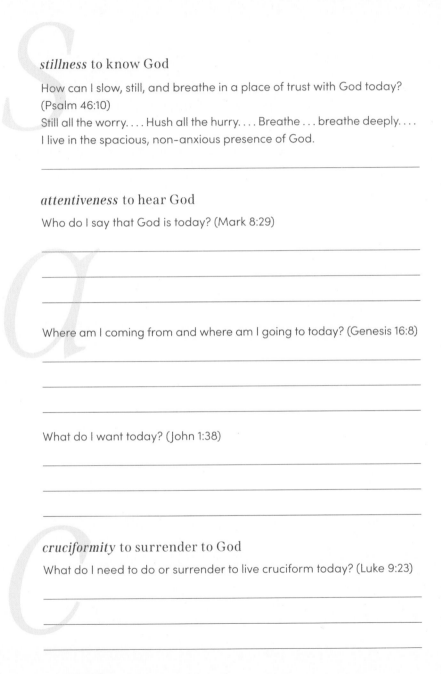

stillness to know God

How can I slow, still, and breathe in a place of trust with God today?
(Psalm 46:10)
Still all the worry.... Hush all the hurry.... Breathe ... breathe deeply....
I live in the spacious, non-anxious presence of God.

_____

attentiveness to hear God

Who do I say that God is today? (Mark 8:29)

_____

_____

_____

Where am I coming from and where am I going to today? (Genesis 16:8)

_____

_____

_____

What do I want today? (John 1:38)

_____

_____

_____

cruciformity to surrender to God

What do I need to do or surrender to live cruciform today? (Luke 9:23)

_____

_____

_____

revelation to see God

How did I experience a fresh revelation from God in His Word today?
(Psalm 119:105)

_____

_____

_____

_____

_____

examine to return to God

What am I afraid of today? (Mark 4:40)

_____

_____

_____

_____

_____

doxology to thank God

What can I thank God for today? (1 Thessalonians 5:18)

_____

_____

_____

What's God inviting me to do today, to make today a day of more
amazing grace?

_____

_____

11

stillness to know God

How can I slow, still, and breathe in a place of trust with God today? (Psalm 46:10)
Still all the worry.... Hush all the hurry.... Breathe ... breathe deeply....
I live in the spacious, non-anxious presence of God.

_____

attentiveness to hear God

Who do I say that God is today? (Mark 8:29)

_____

_____

_____

Where am I coming from and where am I going to today? (Genesis 16:8)

_____

_____

_____

What do I want today? (John 1:38)

_____

_____

_____

cruciformity to surrender to God

What do I need to do or surrender to live cruciform today? (Luke 9:23)

_____

_____

_____

revelation to see God

How did I experience a fresh revelation from God in His Word today?
(Psalm 119:105)

_____

_____

_____

_____

_____

examine to return to God

What am I afraid of today? (Mark 4:40)

_____

_____

_____

_____

doxology to thank God

What can I thank God for today? (1 Thessalonians 5:18)

_____

_____

_____

What's God inviting me to do today, to make today a day of more
amazing grace?

_____

_____

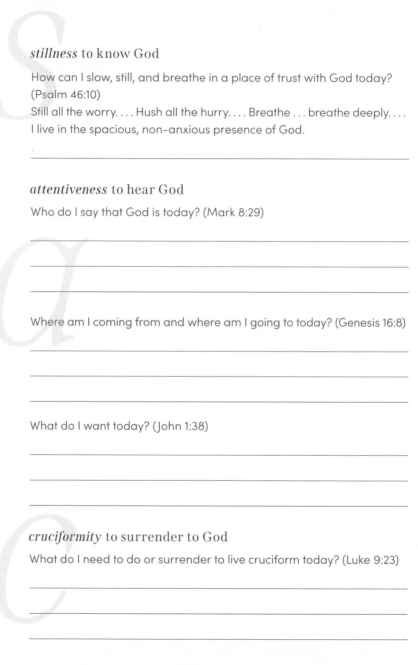

stillness to know God

How can I slow, still, and breathe in a place of trust with God today?
(Psalm 46:10)
Still all the worry.... Hush all the hurry.... Breathe ... breathe deeply....
I live in the spacious, non-anxious presence of God.

_____

attentiveness to hear God

Who do I say that God is today? (Mark 8:29)

_____

_____

_____

Where am I coming from and where am I going to today? (Genesis 16:8)

_____

_____

_____

What do I want today? (John 1:38)

_____

_____

_____

cruciformity to surrender to God

What do I need to do or surrender to live cruciform today? (Luke 9:23)

_____

_____

_____

revelation to see God

How did I experience a fresh revelation from God in His Word today?
(Psalm 119:105)

_____

_____

_____

_____

_____

examine to return to God

What am I afraid of today? (Mark 4:40)

_____

_____

_____

_____

_____

doxology to thank God

What can I thank God for today? (1 Thessalonians 5:18)

_____

_____

_____

What's God inviting me to do today, to make today a day of more
amazing grace?

_____

_____

stillness to know God

How can I slow, still, and breathe in a place of trust with God today?
(Psalm 46:10)
Still all the worry. . . . Hush all the hurry. . . . Breathe . . . breathe deeply. . . .
I live in the spacious, non-anxious presence of God.

_____

attentiveness to hear God

Who do I say that God is today? (Mark 8:29)

_____

_____

_____

Where am I coming from and where am I going to today? (Genesis 16:8)

_____

_____

_____

What do I want today? (John 1:38)

_____

_____

_____

cruciformity to surrender to God

What do I need to do or surrender to live cruciform today? (Luke 9:23)

_____

_____

_____

revelation to see God

How did I experience a fresh revelation from God in His Word today? (Psalm 119:105)

_____

_____

_____

_____

_____

examine to return to God

What am I afraid of today? (Mark 4:40)

_____

_____

_____

_____

_____

doxology to thank God

What can I thank God for today? (1 Thessalonians 5:18)

_____

_____

_____

What's God inviting me to do today, to make today a day of more amazing grace?

_____

_____

stillness to know God

How can I slow, still, and breathe in a place of trust with God today?
(Psalm 46:10)
Still all the worry.... Hush all the hurry.... Breathe ... breathe deeply....
I live in the spacious, non-anxious presence of God.

_____

attentiveness to hear God

Who do I say that God is today? (Mark 8:29)

_____

_____

_____

Where am I coming from and where am I going to today? (Genesis 16:8)

_____

_____

_____

What do I want today? (John 1:38)

_____

_____

_____

cruciformity to surrender to God

What do I need to do or surrender to live cruciform today? (Luke 9:23)

_____

_____

_____

revelation to see God

How did I experience a fresh revelation from God in His Word today?
(Psalm 119:105)

_____

_____

_____

_____

_____

examine to return to God

What am I afraid of today? (Mark 4:40)

_____

_____

_____

_____

doxology to thank God

What can I thank God for today? (1 Thessalonians 5:18)

_____

_____

_____

What's God inviting me to do today, to make today a day of more
amazing grace?

_____

_____

stillness to know God

How can I slow, still, and breathe in a place of trust with God today?
(Psalm 46:10)
Still all the worry. . . . Hush all the hurry. . . . Breathe . . . breathe deeply. . . .
I live in the spacious, non-anxious presence of God.

_____

attentiveness to hear God

Who do I say that God is today? (Mark 8:29)

_____

_____

_____

Where am I coming from and where am I going to today? (Genesis 16:8)

_____

_____

_____

What do I want today? (John 1:38)

_____

_____

_____

cruciformity to surrender to God

What do I need to do or surrender to live cruciform today? (Luke 9:23)

_____

_____

_____

DAY 7

revelation to see God

How did I experience a fresh revelation from God in His Word today? (Psalm 119:105)

_____
_____
_____
_____
_____

examine to return to God

What am I afraid of today? (Mark 4:40)

_____
_____
_____
_____

doxology to thank God

What can I thank God for today? (1 Thessalonians 5:18)

_____
_____
_____

What's God inviting me to do today, to make today a day of more amazing grace?

_____
_____

21

stillness to know God

How can I slow, still, and breathe in a place of trust with God today? (Psalm 46:10)

Still all the worry.... Hush all the hurry.... Breathe ... breathe deeply.... I live in the spacious, non-anxious presence of God.

_____

attentiveness to hear God

Who do I say that God is today? (Mark 8:29)

_____

_____

_____

Where am I coming from and where am I going to today? (Genesis 16:8)

_____

_____

_____

What do I want today? (John 1:38)

_____

_____

_____

cruciformity to surrender to God

What do I need to do or surrender to live cruciform today? (Luke 9:23)

_____

_____

revelation to see God

How did I experience a fresh revelation from God in His Word today?
(Psalm 119:105)

_____

_____

_____

_____

_____

examine to return to God

What am I afraid of today? (Mark 4:40)

_____

_____

_____

_____

doxology to thank God

What can I thank God for today? (1 Thessalonians 5:18)

_____

_____

_____

What's God inviting me to do today, to make today a day of more
amazing grace?

_____

_____

stillness to know God

How can I slow, still, and breathe in a place of trust with God today?
(Psalm 46:10)
Still all the worry.... Hush all the hurry.... Breathe ... breathe deeply....
I live in the spacious, non-anxious presence of God.

_____

attentiveness to hear God

Who do I say that God is today? (Mark 8:29)

_____

_____

_____

Where am I coming from and where am I going to today? (Genesis 16:8)

_____

_____

_____

What do I want today? (John 1:38)

_____

_____

_____

cruciformity to surrender to God

What do I need to do or surrender to live cruciform today? (Luke 9:23)

_____

_____

_____

revelation to see God

How did I experience a fresh revelation from God in His Word today? (Psalm 119:105)

_____

_____

_____

_____

_____

examine to return to God

What am I afraid of today? (Mark 4:40)

_____

_____

_____

_____

_____

doxology to thank God

What can I thank God for today? (1 Thessalonians 5:18)

_____

_____

_____

What's God inviting me to do today, to make today a day of more amazing grace?

_____

_____

stillness to know God

How can I slow, still, and breathe in a place of trust with God today?
(Psalm 46:10)
Still all the worry.... Hush all the hurry.... Breathe ... breathe deeply....
I live in the spacious, non-anxious presence of God.

_____

attentiveness to hear God

Who do I say that God is today? (Mark 8:29)

_____

_____

_____

Where am I coming from and where am I going to today? (Genesis 16:8)

_____

_____

_____

What do I want today? (John 1:38)

_____

_____

_____

cruciformity to surrender to God

What do I need to do or surrender to live cruciform today? (Luke 9:23)

_____

_____

_____

revelation to see God

How did I experience a fresh revelation from God in His Word today?
(Psalm 119:105)

_____

_____

_____

_____

_____

examine to return to God

What am I afraid of today? (Mark 4:40)

_____

_____

_____

_____

doxology to thank God

What can I thank God for today? (1 Thessalonians 5:18)

_____

_____

_____

What's God inviting me to do today, to make today a day of more
amazing grace?

_____

_____

stillness to know God

How can I slow, still, and breathe in a place of trust with God today?
(Psalm 46:10)
Still all the worry.... Hush all the hurry.... Breathe ... breathe deeply....
I live in the spacious, non-anxious presence of God.

_____

attentiveness to hear God

Who do I say that God is today? (Mark 8:29)

_____

_____

_____

Where am I coming from and where am I going to today? (Genesis 16:8)

_____

_____

_____

What do I want today? (John 1:38)

_____

_____

_____

cruciformity to surrender to God

What do I need to do or surrender to live cruciform today? (Luke 9:23)

_____

_____

_____

revelation to see God

How did I experience a fresh revelation from God in His Word today?
(Psalm 119:105)

_____

_____

_____

_____

_____

examine to return to God

What am I afraid of today? (Mark 4:40)

_____

_____

_____

_____

_____

doxology to thank God

What can I thank God for today? (1 Thessalonians 5:18)

_____

_____

_____

What's God inviting me to do today, to make today a day of more
amazing grace?

_____

_____

stillness to know God

How can I slow, still, and breathe in a place of trust with God today?
(Psalm 46:10)
Still all the worry. . . . Hush all the hurry. . . . Breathe . . . breathe deeply. . . .
I live in the spacious, non-anxious presence of God.

_____

attentiveness to hear God

Who do I say that God is today? (Mark 8:29)

_____

_____

_____

Where am I coming from and where am I going to today? (Genesis 16:8)

_____

_____

_____

What do I want today? (John 1:38)

_____

_____

_____

cruciformity to surrender to God

What do I need to do or surrender to live cruciform today? (Luke 9:23)

_____

_____

_____

revelation to see God

How did I experience a fresh revelation from God in His Word today?
(Psalm 119:105)

_____

_____

_____

_____

_____

examine to return to God

What am I afraid of today? (Mark 4:40)

_____

_____

_____

_____

_____

doxology to thank God

What can I thank God for today? (1 Thessalonians 5:18)

_____

_____

_____

What's God inviting me to do today, to make today a day of more
amazing grace?

_____

_____

stillness to know God

How can I slow, still, and breathe in a place of trust with God today?
(Psalm 46:10)
Still all the worry.... Hush all the hurry.... Breathe ... breathe deeply....
I live in the spacious, non-anxious presence of God.

_____

attentiveness to hear God

Who do I say that God is today? (Mark 8:29)

_____

_____

_____

Where am I coming from and where am I going to today? (Genesis 16:8)

_____

_____

_____

What do I want today? (John 1:38)

_____

_____

_____

cruciformity to surrender to God

What do I need to do or surrender to live cruciform today? (Luke 9:23)

_____

_____

_____

revelation to see God

How did I experience a fresh revelation from God in His Word today?
(Psalm 119:105)

_____

_____

_____

_____

_____

examine to return to God

What am I afraid of today? (Mark 4:40)

_____

_____

_____

_____

doxology to thank God

What can I thank God for today? (1 Thessalonians 5:18)

_____

_____

What's God inviting me to do today, to make today a day of more
amazing grace?

_____

_____

stillness to know God

How can I slow, still, and breathe in a place of trust with God today?
(Psalm 46:10)
Still all the worry. . . . Hush all the hurry. . . . Breathe . . . breathe deeply. . . .
I live in the spacious, non-anxious presence of God.

_____

attentiveness to hear God

Who do I say that God is today? (Mark 8:29)

_____

_____

_____

Where am I coming from and where am I going to today? (Genesis 16:8)

_____

_____

_____

What do I want today? (John 1:38)

_____

_____

_____

cruciformity to surrender to God

What do I need to do or surrender to live cruciform today? (Luke 9:23)

_____

_____

_____

revelation to see God

How did I experience a fresh revelation from God in His Word today? (Psalm 119:105)

_____

_____

_____

_____

_____

examine to return to God

What am I afraid of today? (Mark 4:40)

_____

_____

_____

_____

doxology to thank God

What can I thank God for today? (1 Thessalonians 5:18)

_____

_____

_____

What's God inviting me to do today, to make today a day of more amazing grace?

_____

_____

stillness to know God

How can I slow, still, and breathe in a place of trust with God today?
(Psalm 46:10)
Still all the worry.... Hush all the hurry.... Breathe ... breathe deeply....
I live in the spacious, non-anxious presence of God.

---

attentiveness to hear God

Who do I say that God is today? (Mark 8:29)

Where am I coming from and where am I going to today? (Genesis 16:8)

What do I want today? (John 1:38)

---

cruciformity to surrender to God

What do I need to do or surrender to live cruciform today? (Luke 9:23)

---

revelation to see God

How did I experience a fresh revelation from God in His Word today? (Psalm 119:105)

_____

_____

_____

_____

_____

examine to return to God

What am I afraid of today? (Mark 4:40)

_____

_____

_____

_____

doxology to thank God

What can I thank God for today? (1 Thessalonians 5:18)

_____

_____

_____

What's God inviting me to do today, to make today a day of more amazing grace?

_____

_____

Attentiveness

When you are yearning to have a relationship with God, your sacred work is to still long enough to pay attention and locate your soul—so you can know where you are in relation *to God.* The holy work of being human is to keep paying attention to the location of our own souls: *location, location, location.* And then *attention, attention, attention*—to what is happening *within* our own souls.

What we pay attention to is how we spend our lives. Pay attention mostly to the news—and we can end up spending our one life on headlines. Pay attention mostly to screens—and we can spend most of our days in a digital haze. Pay attention mostly to the negative—and we spend the only life we have on the very things that we wish weren't.

As it turns out—we gain more of whatever we pay attention to.

Pay attention to love—and you are given more love. Pay attention to the good and the beautiful—and you spend your soul on what is good and beautiful. Pay attention to sunrises and laughter; pay attention to smiles and patches of light on the floor; pay attention to God in the everyday moments. *So the question is: What do you really want more of?*

Attend to God—this is the best way to tend to your own soul.

If you stilled your soul right now, could you attend to the voice of God speaking directly to you?

> If you receive my words and treasure up my commandments with
> you, making your ear attentive to wisdom and inclining your heart to

understanding; yes, if you call out for insight and raise your voice for understanding, if you seek it like silver and search for it as for hidden treasures, then you will understand the fear of the LORD and find the knowledge of God (Proverbs 2:1–5 ESV).

Therefore we must pay much closer attention to what we have heard, lest we drift away from it (Hebrews 2:1 ESV).

Without daily attentiveness to the way of Jesus Himself, to the questions of Jesus—it's our default to drift away. Therapist Curt Thompson asks in *The Soul of Shame*: Isn't God asking questions of us all the time?[1] God's voice still reverberates across time and wakes our souls.

- "Where are you?" God called in the garden, the One always looking for the way to us (Genesis 3:9).
- "Who do you say I am?" Jesus questioned Peter (Luke 9:20).
- "What do you want?" Jesus asked His disciples (John 1:38).
- "Where have you come from, and where are you going?" the angel of the Lord asked a fleeing Hagar (Genesis 16:8).

Maybe if we begin to attend to, to answer, God's questions, we'd be less likely to question God's ways.

Right now, that your soul might not drift away, attend to who your soul says God is. That is what God is asking you right in this moment: "Who do you say I am?" (Matthew 16:15). The answer to this question matters—perhaps more than any other question. "What comes into our minds when we think about God is the most important thing about us," writes A. W. Tozer.[2] *Whoever you say He is determines the way your life will go.* Say He is failing at being a good God—and your life ultimately fails to go a good way. Say He is a kind God—and your soul flourishes in the kinds of ways you always hoped.

Pay attention to the kindness of God—and you find the way to the kind of life you always dreamed of.

It is paramount that you pay attention to who you say God is—because who you say God is determines if you will spend your life in deep joy or deep in a wilderness of bewilderment. Attentiveness to the kindness of who God is leads to the remembrance of all His loving-kindness, and in turn, this attentiveness acts as a compass in your soul, turning you toward all kinds of moments of grace on the way. *Pay attention, soul.*

- Who do you say God is?
- How will you still your soul and allow God to attend to you?

Everything else can follow after—everything can be attended to after we give attention to the One who so tenderly attends to us, so lovingly attaches Himself to us. He is not a distant God, but a God who pulls you in so close that the calming and regulating rhythm of His heartbeat calms yours. His attention is not divided, not pulled into many directions like ours. His attention is fixed fully on you.

The only way a heart can ever be unafraid and untroubled is for it to be undivided. How can we beg God to divide seas for us if our own attention is divided? Why expect God to split waters for us if we are just giving Him our split attention? The only way our waves can be divided is to give God our undivided attention.

Do you hear it right now, in the stillness of your soul as you pause: the Lord calling after you, asking you to attend to where your heart really is, where your soul really is, like He called after Hagar? "Where have you come from, and where are you going?" (Genesis 16:8).

Unless we make paying attention to where our souls are our everyday way of life, how can we really know where we are going or coming from—and how will we see the way through? Attend to where your soul is. God is here in this sacred place right now, waiting to hear your whole honest heart in prayer.

- Where are you? Where are you in relation to Him?
- Where have you been of late?
- Where in your life are you coming from a place of worry and fear?
- Where are you coming from, in your mind, in your day, in your soul, when you're paying attention to what seems to be going wrong, all that seems to be in the way? In what ways could you pay attention to grace?

Jesus, in His own desperate hour, in His Gethsemane, turned His eyes from the horrors of where He'd come from and looked to where He was going and "lifted up his eyes to heaven, and said, 'Father, the hour has come; glorify your Son that the Son may glorify you'" (John 17:1 ESV).

In this holy and hurting moment, in the middle of the world's mourning, in the middle of our own chaos, in all our own hurting ways, from wherever we are coming—right now, we lift our eyes up to where we are going, and we pray: *Father—the hour has come. The hour when I need You to come through, to show me where I am going, how to live the way, to turn my eyes to rest in Yours, my only way—help me glorify You.*

Your life goes where you keep looking. Looking around at everything and everyone else can cause all kinds of heartache. *Looking up heals all kinds of heartache.*

And the old hymn resonates in our aching, praying hearts:

"Turn your eyes upon Jesus, look full in His wonderful face, and the things of earth will grow strangely dim, in the light of His glory and grace."

- What are you, and your soul, attending to today?
- Where is your gaze directed and drawn to?
- What holds your heart's attention today? How does your day keep turning to face God—or how and where does it turn in another direction?
- How could you look long on Jesus today? Because whatever we look at is what we become.
- How could you gaze on the cross of love today? Because whatever we look at is what we become.
- How could you keep looking for the goodness and the beauty and the loveliness and the mercy and all these gifts of grace? Because whatever we look at is what we become.
- Where are you paying attention to the kindness of God in your life?

C. S. Lewis says: "To a man on a mountain road by night, a glimpse of the next three feet of road may matter more than a vision of the horizon."[3] Don't be overwhelmed by the darkness or the night; keep your eyes fixed on the next three feet ahead. Like a lantern in a darkened valley, the Way Himself breaks through the darkness every time. Step by step, a shattering of darkness, because even the dark is not dark in Him (Psalm 139:12).

And maybe even more important than where you are going—pay attention to Who you are going with. Because when you know the One who knows you more than you know yourself, you can trust that no matter where you end up, *you will always be seen, chosen, and loved.* Just for today, *do not worry* about what the road ahead holds—just pay attention to the One who holds your heart.

> "Give your entire attention to what God is doing right now, and don't get worked up about what may or may not happen tomorrow. God will help you deal with whatever hard things come up when the time comes" (Matthew 6:34 MSG).

> So here's what [to do]. . . . Take your everyday, ordinary life—your sleeping, eating, going-to-work, and walking-around life—and place it before God as an offering. Embracing what God does for you is the best thing you can do for him. . . . Fix your attention on God. You'll be changed from the inside out (Romans 12:1–2 MSG).

It's this fixing your attention on God in the everyday things that begins to fix your heart to God, which profoundly changes your perspective on the problems of the everyday things. Sometimes the best training for the really big things is to practice paying attention to God through the little everyday things.

"The way to life—to God!—is vigorous and requires total attention," says Jesus in Matthew 7:14 (MSG).

While you may not see the horizon right now, He can, and He is walking with you no matter what that horizon looks like. Attend to where you are in relation to Him, and you'll see the way forward: *intimate relationship with Him.*

After we first attend to gazing on who we say God is, which tends to shape every other aspect of our life, then we attend to where our soul truly is coming from and where our soul is actually going—which tends to determine the very direction of our day, the actual trajectory of the roads through our own mind and heart and soul. That way, we can finally attend to Jesus' heart-probing question of us: "What do you want?" (Matthew 20:32).

It can strike us as a strange question. *Are we allowed to attend to what we actually want?* It is our Lord, King Jesus, who asks the question of us, so this is a question we not only can, but need, to ask our own soul: *What do you want?*

What we want—becomes who we are.

What we want—shapes our way.

What we want—reveals the way of our heart.

What we want—can become what we worship.

It was John Calvin who wrote that the human heart is a perpetual idol factory—and he is not wrong. Naming our wants can be about naming our idols. Name your wants—and you can begin to slay your idols.

And yet this is also just as true and powerful:

The King of the universe attends to your wants.

Jesus asks what we want because He wants us to know He cares about what we want. God attends to your wants because He never stops attending to you.

Your God, He sees, and He is calling out your name. Gaze long at the Way Himself—and you'll find a way you never dreamed of. Attend to who your soul says God is, where you are coming from and where you are going, and what you really want.

Morning prayer and devotions can become all-day prayer and devotions . . . when we choose to keep paying attention to God.

Devotion grows toward whatever you pay attention to.

Here is sacred, now is holy, and He beckons you to come.

stillness to know God

How can I slow, still, and breathe in a place of trust with God today?
(Psalm 46:10)
Still all the worry.... Hush all the hurry.... Breathe ... breathe deeply....
I live in the spacious, non-anxious presence of God.

_____

attentiveness to hear God

Who do I say that God is today? (Mark 8:29)

_____

_____

_____

Where am I coming from and where am I going to today? (Genesis 16:8)

_____

_____

_____

What do I want today? (John 1:38)

_____

_____

_____

cruciformity to surrender to God

What do I need to do or surrender to live cruciform today? (Luke 9:23)

_____

_____

_____

revelation to see God

How did I experience a fresh revelation from God in His Word today?
(Psalm 119:105)

_____

_____

_____

_____

_____

examine to return to God

What am I afraid of today? (Mark 4:40)

_____

_____

_____

_____

doxology to thank God

What can I thank God for today? (1 Thessalonians 5:18)

_____

_____

_____

What's God inviting me to do today, to make today a day of more
amazing grace?

_____

_____

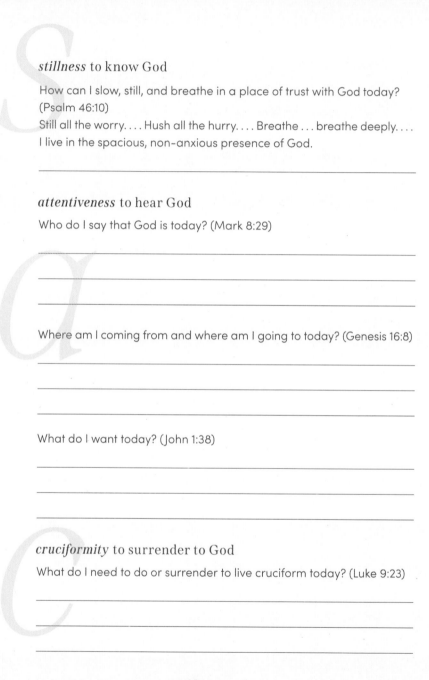

stillness to know God

How can I slow, still, and breathe in a place of trust with God today? (Psalm 46:10)
Still all the worry. . . . Hush all the hurry. . . . Breathe . . . breathe deeply. . . .
I live in the spacious, non-anxious presence of God.

_____

attentiveness to hear God

Who do I say that God is today? (Mark 8:29)

_____

_____

_____

Where am I coming from and where am I going to today? (Genesis 16:8)

_____

_____

_____

What do I want today? (John 1:38)

_____

_____

_____

cruciformity to surrender to God

What do I need to do or surrender to live cruciform today? (Luke 9:23)

_____

_____

_____

revelation to see God

How did I experience a fresh revelation from God in His Word today? (Psalm 119:105)

_____

_____

_____

_____

_____

examine to return to God

What am I afraid of today? (Mark 4:40)

_____

_____

_____

_____

doxology to thank God

What can I thank God for today? (1 Thessalonians 5:18)

_____

_____

_____

What's God inviting me to do today, to make today a day of more amazing grace?

_____

_____

stillness to know God

How can I slow, still, and breathe in a place of trust with God today?
(Psalm 46:10)
Still all the worry.... Hush all the hurry.... Breathe ... breathe deeply....
I live in the spacious, non-anxious presence of God.

_____

attentiveness to hear God

Who do I say that God is today? (Mark 8:29)

_____

_____

_____

Where am I coming from and where am I going to today? (Genesis 16:8)

_____

_____

_____

What do I want today? (John 1:38)

_____

_____

_____

cruciformity to surrender to God

What do I need to do or surrender to live cruciform today? (Luke 9:23)

_____

_____

_____

revelation to see God

How did I experience a fresh revelation from God in His Word today? (Psalm 119:105)

_____

_____

_____

_____

_____

examine to return to God

What am I afraid of today? (Mark 4:40)

_____

_____

_____

_____

doxology to thank God

What can I thank God for today? (1 Thessalonians 5:18)

_____

_____

_____

What's God inviting me to do today, to make today a day of more amazing grace?

_____

_____

stillness to know God

How can I slow, still, and breathe in a place of trust with God today?
(Psalm 46:10)
Still all the worry. . . . Hush all the hurry. . . . Breathe . . . breathe deeply. . . .
I live in the spacious, non-anxious presence of God.

_____

attentiveness to hear God

Who do I say that God is today? (Mark 8:29)

_____

_____

_____

Where am I coming from and where am I going to today? (Genesis 16:8)

_____

_____

_____

What do I want today? (John 1:38)

_____

_____

_____

cruciformity to surrender to God

What do I need to do or surrender to live cruciform today? (Luke 9:23)

_____

_____

_____

revelation to see God

How did I experience a fresh revelation from God in His Word today?
(Psalm 119:105)

_____

_____

_____

_____

_____

examine to return to God

What am I afraid of today? (Mark 4:40)

_____

_____

_____

_____

doxology to thank God

What can I thank God for today? (1 Thessalonians 5:18)

_____

_____

_____

What's God inviting me to do today, to make today a day of more
amazing grace?

_____

_____

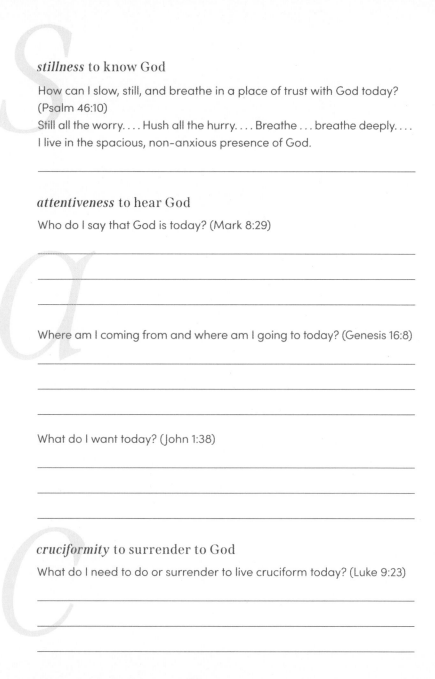

stillness to know God

How can I slow, still, and breathe in a place of trust with God today? (Psalm 46:10)
Still all the worry. . . . Hush all the hurry. . . . Breathe . . . breathe deeply. . . .
I live in the spacious, non-anxious presence of God.

_____

attentiveness to hear God

Who do I say that God is today? (Mark 8:29)

_____

_____

_____

Where am I coming from and where am I going to today? (Genesis 16:8)

_____

_____

_____

What do I want today? (John 1:38)

_____

_____

_____

cruciformity to surrender to God

What do I need to do or surrender to live cruciform today? (Luke 9:23)

_____

_____

_____

revelation to see God

How did I experience a fresh revelation from God in His Word today? (Psalm 119:105)

_____

_____

_____

_____

_____

examine to return to God

What am I afraid of today? (Mark 4:40)

_____

_____

_____

_____

doxology to thank God

What can I thank God for today? (1 Thessalonians 5:18)

_____

_____

_____

What's God inviting me to do today, to make today a day of more amazing grace?

_____

_____

stillness to know God

How can I slow, still, and breathe in a place of trust with God today?
(Psalm 46:10)
Still all the worry.... Hush all the hurry.... Breathe ... breathe deeply....
I live in the spacious, non-anxious presence of God.

_____

attentiveness to hear God

Who do I say that God is today? (Mark 8:29)

_____

_____

_____

Where am I coming from and where am I going to today? (Genesis 16:8)

_____

_____

_____

What do I want today? (John 1:38)

_____

_____

_____

cruciformity to surrender to God

What do I need to do or surrender to live cruciform today? (Luke 9:23)

_____

_____

_____

revelation to see God

How did I experience a fresh revelation from God in His Word today?
(Psalm 119:105)

_____

_____

_____

_____

_____

examine to return to God

What am I afraid of today? (Mark 4:40)

_____

_____

_____

_____

doxology to thank God

What can I thank God for today? (1 Thessalonians 5:18)

_____

_____

_____

What's God inviting me to do today, to make today a day of more
amazing grace?

_____

_____

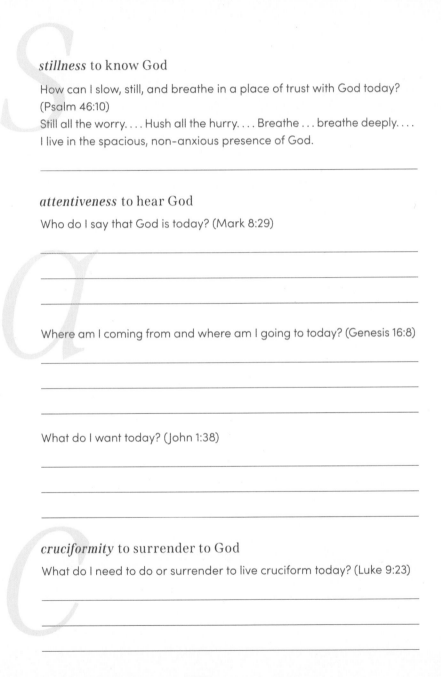

stillness to know God

How can I slow, still, and breathe in a place of trust with God today?
(Psalm 46:10)
Still all the worry.... Hush all the hurry.... Breathe ... breathe deeply....
I live in the spacious, non-anxious presence of God.

_____

attentiveness to hear God

Who do I say that God is today? (Mark 8:29)

_____

_____

_____

Where am I coming from and where am I going to today? (Genesis 16:8)

_____

_____

_____

What do I want today? (John 1:38)

_____

_____

_____

cruciformity to surrender to God

What do I need to do or surrender to live cruciform today? (Luke 9:23)

_____

_____

_____

revelation to see God

How did I experience a fresh revelation from God in His Word today?
(Psalm 119:105)

_____

_____

_____

_____

_____

examine to return to God

What am I afraid of today? (Mark 4:40)

_____

_____

_____

_____

_____

doxology to thank God

What can I thank God for today? (1 Thessalonians 5:18)

_____

_____

_____

What's God inviting me to do today, to make today a day of more
amazing grace?

_____

_____

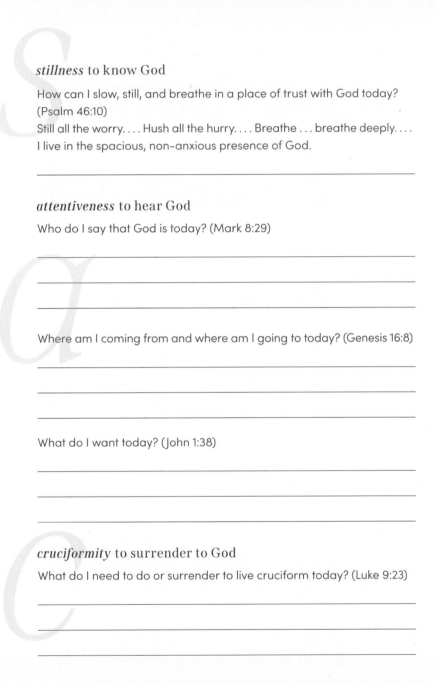

stillness to know God

How can I slow, still, and breathe in a place of trust with God today?
(Psalm 46:10)
Still all the worry. . . . Hush all the hurry. . . . Breathe . . . breathe deeply. . . .
I live in the spacious, non-anxious presence of God.

_____

attentiveness to hear God

Who do I say that God is today? (Mark 8:29)

_____

_____

_____

Where am I coming from and where am I going to today? (Genesis 16:8)

_____

_____

_____

What do I want today? (John 1:38)

_____

_____

_____

cruciformity to surrender to God

What do I need to do or surrender to live cruciform today? (Luke 9:23)

_____

_____

_____

revelation to see God

How did I experience a fresh revelation from God in His Word today?
(Psalm 119:105)

_____

_____

_____

_____

_____

examine to return to God

What am I afraid of today? (Mark 4:40)

_____

_____

_____

_____

_____

doxology to thank God

What can I thank God for today? (1 Thessalonians 5:18)

_____

_____

_____

What's God inviting me to do today, to make today a day of more
amazing grace?

_____

_____

stillness to know God

How can I slow, still, and breathe in a place of trust with God today?
(Psalm 46:10)
Still all the worry.... Hush all the hurry.... Breathe ... breathe deeply....
I live in the spacious, non-anxious presence of God.

_____

attentiveness to hear God

Who do I say that God is today? (Mark 8:29)

_____

_____

_____

Where am I coming from and where am I going to today? (Genesis 16:8)

_____

_____

_____

What do I want today? (John 1:38)

_____

_____

_____

cruciformity to surrender to God

What do I need to do or surrender to live cruciform today? (Luke 9:23)

_____

_____

_____

revelation to see God

How did I experience a fresh revelation from God in His Word today?
(Psalm 119:105)

_____

_____

_____

_____

_____

examine to return to God

What am I afraid of today? (Mark 4:40)

_____

_____

_____

_____

_____

doxology to thank God

What can I thank God for today? (1 Thessalonians 5:18)

_____

_____

_____

What's God inviting me to do today, to make today a day of more
amazing grace?

_____

_____

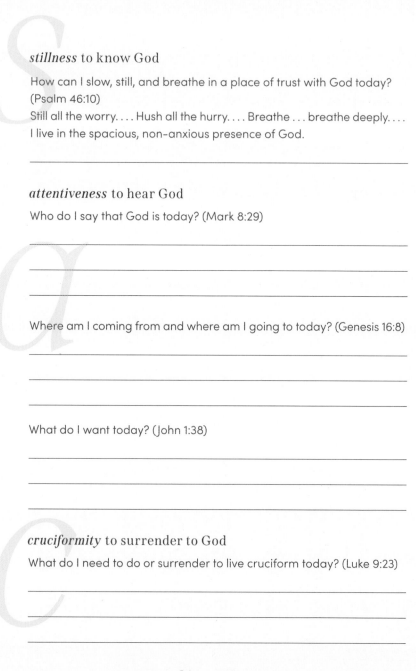

stillness to know God

How can I slow, still, and breathe in a place of trust with God today?
(Psalm 46:10)
Still all the worry.... Hush all the hurry.... Breathe ... breathe deeply....
I live in the spacious, non-anxious presence of God.

_____

attentiveness to hear God

Who do I say that God is today? (Mark 8:29)

_____

_____

_____

Where am I coming from and where am I going to today? (Genesis 16:8)

_____

_____

_____

What do I want today? (John 1:38)

_____

_____

_____

cruciformity to surrender to God

What do I need to do or surrender to live cruciform today? (Luke 9:23)

_____

_____

_____

revelation to see God

How did I experience a fresh revelation from God in His Word today? (Psalm 119:105)

_____

_____

_____

_____

_____

examine to return to God

What am I afraid of today? (Mark 4:40)

_____

_____

_____

_____

doxology to thank God

What can I thank God for today? (1 Thessalonians 5:18)

_____

_____

_____

What's God inviting me to do today, to make today a day of more amazing grace?

_____

_____

stillness to know God

How can I slow, still, and breathe in a place of trust with God today?
(Psalm 46:10)
Still all the worry.... Hush all the hurry.... Breathe ... breathe deeply....
I live in the spacious, non-anxious presence of God.

_____

attentiveness to hear God

Who do I say that God is today? (Mark 8:29)

_____

_____

_____

Where am I coming from and where am I going to today? (Genesis 16:8)

_____

_____

_____

What do I want today? (John 1:38)

_____

_____

_____

cruciformity to surrender to God

What do I need to do or surrender to live cruciform today? (Luke 9:23)

_____

_____

_____

revelation to see God

How did I experience a fresh revelation from God in His Word today? (Psalm 119:105)

_____

_____

_____

_____

_____

examine to return to God

What am I afraid of today? (Mark 4:40)

_____

_____

_____

_____

doxology to thank God

What can I thank God for today? (1 Thessalonians 5:18)

_____

_____

_____

What's God inviting me to do today, to make today a day of more amazing grace?

_____

_____

stillness to know God

How can I slow, still, and breathe in a place of trust with God today? (Psalm 46:10)
Still all the worry.... Hush all the hurry.... Breathe ... breathe deeply....
I live in the spacious, non-anxious presence of God.

_____

attentiveness to hear God

Who do I say that God is today? (Mark 8:29)

_____

_____

_____

Where am I coming from and where am I going to today? (Genesis 16:8)

_____

_____

_____

What do I want today? (John 1:38)

_____

_____

_____

cruciformity to surrender to God

What do I need to do or surrender to live cruciform today? (Luke 9:23)

_____

_____

_____

revelation to see God

How did I experience a fresh revelation from God in His Word today? (Psalm 119:105)

_____

_____

_____

_____

_____

examine to return to God

What am I afraid of today? (Mark 4:40)

_____

_____

_____

_____

doxology to thank God

What can I thank God for today? (1 Thessalonians 5:18)

_____

_____

_____

What's God inviting me to do today, to make today a day of more amazing grace?

_____

_____

stillness to know God

How can I slow, still, and breathe in a place of trust with God today? (Psalm 46:10)
Still all the worry. . . . Hush all the hurry. . . . Breathe . . . breathe deeply. . . . I live in the spacious, non-anxious presence of God.

_____

attentiveness to hear God

Who do I say that God is today? (Mark 8:29)

_____

_____

_____

Where am I coming from and where am I going to today? (Genesis 16:8)

_____

_____

_____

What do I want today? (John 1:38)

_____

_____

_____

cruciformity to surrender to God

What do I need to do or surrender to live cruciform today? (Luke 9:23)

_____

_____

revelation to see God

How did I experience a fresh revelation from God in His Word today?
(Psalm 119:105)

_____

_____

_____

_____

_____

examine to return to God

What am I afraid of today? (Mark 4:40)

_____

_____

_____

_____

_____

doxology to thank God

What can I thank God for today? (1 Thessalonians 5:18)

_____

_____

_____

What's God inviting me to do today, to make today a day of more
amazing grace?

_____

_____

stillness to know God

How can I slow, still, and breathe in a place of trust with God today?
(Psalm 46:10)
Still all the worry. . . . Hush all the hurry. . . . Breathe . . . breathe deeply. . . .
I live in the spacious, non-anxious presence of God.

---

attentiveness to hear God

Who do I say that God is today? (Mark 8:29)

Where am I coming from and where am I going to today? (Genesis 16:8)

What do I want today? (John 1:38)

---

cruciformity to surrender to God

What do I need to do or surrender to live cruciform today? (Luke 9:23)

---

revelation to see God

How did I experience a fresh revelation from God in His Word today? (Psalm 119:105)

_____

_____

_____

_____

_____

examine to return to God

What am I afraid of today? (Mark 4:40)

_____

_____

_____

_____

doxology to thank God

What can I thank God for today? (1 Thessalonians 5:18)

_____

_____

_____

What's God inviting me to do today, to make today a day of more amazing grace?

_____

_____

stillness to know God

How can I slow, still, and breathe in a place of trust with God today?
(Psalm 46:10)
Still all the worry. . . . Hush all the hurry. . . . Breathe . . . breathe deeply. . . .
I live in the spacious, non-anxious presence of God.

_____

attentiveness to hear God

Who do I say that God is today? (Mark 8:29)

_____

_____

_____

Where am I coming from and where am I going to today? (Genesis 16:8)

_____

_____

_____

What do I want today? (John 1:38)

_____

_____

_____

cruciformity to surrender to God

What do I need to do or surrender to live cruciform today? (Luke 9:23)

_____

_____

_____

revelation to see God

How did I experience a fresh revelation from God in His Word today?
(Psalm 119:105)

_____

_____

_____

_____

_____

examine to return to God

What am I afraid of today? (Mark 4:40)

_____

_____

_____

_____

_____

doxology to thank God

What can I thank God for today? (1 Thessalonians 5:18)

_____

_____

_____

What's God inviting me to do today, to make today a day of more
amazing grace?

_____

_____

Cruciformity is everything.

The whole practice of Christianity is the practice of cruciformity.

To form your life into the shape of a cross is to live like Christ, to live with your arms stretched wide open, to let go of all forms of control, to live with your vulnerable heart exposed, to love vulnerably enough to be hurt—this cruciformity is what love is.

When we commit to picking up our cross and living cruciform—this is when all of life begins to transform.

This is a profoundly countercultural, sacred way to live, because this is our Father's world, and in our Father's world, living cruciform is the greatest form of supernatural power. The way of Jesus is never about upward mobility but always about the way deeper down, the way of the cross, the way of cruciformity toward God-intimacy.

Cruciformity is always the healing trajectory toward intimacy.

At every crossroad of our lives, the call is to remember the direction of the Way Himself, whom we follow. He carries a cross and is going the way that will pass through suffering, toward a place of dying, to bring about the greatest joy of rising. Every real map will point the unexpected way toward joy: Gethsemanes are places of intimacy. Why expect another trajectory when you're following a suffering Savior?

If we want our WayMaking God to make a way, we need to trust that His life-giving way in our lives always runs through seasons and valleys of suffering; He has no other way. Not because He doesn't love us, *but exactly because He does*. Because "suffering produces endurance, and endurance produces character, and character produces hope, and hope does not put us to shame, because God's love has been poured into our hearts through the Holy Spirit who has been given to us" (Romans 5:3–5 ESV). The suffering Savior wants nothing less than to be with us, and valleys of suffering is the way He is for us, near us, and in us, and tenderly, powerfully grows us more into wholeness and into the image of Himself.

This journey of being on the way with Jesus, with the suffering Savior who picks up a cross and carries our brokenness and sinfulness to Calvary—this way of carrying our cross, of being shaped and formed like a cross, carries us into a kind of holy of holies.

Can you still your heart right now and move into a posture of cruciformity—hands and arms wide open? This work of surrender, this is a daily, hard, and holy sacred work.

Sometimes surrender feels like an undoing—because, in a way, it is exactly that. It is an undoing of ourselves, an unfurling of our hearts. It is an opening up of our hearts, an opening up of our hands, our arms, our lives. And sometimes . . . sometimes surrender is exhausting. And we fail, and fall, and falter, and flail around in our attempts to surrender. We open up our hearts and then recoil from vulnerability with others and our Lord out of fear of being rejected, forsaken. This way of cruciformity—to vulnerability, to intimacy—can feel terrifying. But just as we could not fulfill our own salvation upon that cross, we cannot fulfill a life of cruciformity or surrender on our own.

Jesus lived with arms wide open so that we could too.

Jesus' arms are always stretched wide open to wrap us in His cruciform love, so we are safe to live into a wide-open, cruciform surrender too.

Cruciformity is everything because the form of the cross is the form of all our hope in suffering, the form of the exodus from every impossibility, the form of our whole answer to the problem of evil: God Himself has entered this suffering world, and He went to the cross to absorb every atom of it.

The cross proves we aren't alone in our suffering; the cross proves God feels it all too.

True life transformation happens whenever a life chooses cruciformation—chooses to enter into the sufferings of Christ—because if you "partake of the sufferings of Christ, rejoice that when his glory shall be revealed, you may also be glad with exceeding joy" (1 Peter 4:13 DRA).

To form your days cruciform is to choose nothing less than to "share his sufferings, becoming like him in his death, that by any means possible [you] may attain the resurrection from the dead" (Philippians 3:10–11 ESV). Cruciformity is the everything that beats at the heart of Christianity: "We always carry around in our body the death of Jesus, so that the life of Jesus may also be revealed in our body" (2 Corinthians 4:10 NIV).

All of life turns on the turn. And wherever there is turning and curving inward, there is never healthy growth, rather, this is exactly how the soul becomes painfully ingrown.

Cruciformity forms us into who we always were meant to be.

To live cruciform, to reach out toward others, toward God—this is the posture of health, of growth. Set your life on the way of being cruciform, and you will always have a growth mindset.

- What is one place in your life today where Jesus is asking you to open wide your arms, your heart, and live cruciform? Surrendered? Open? With vulnerability that leads to true intimacy?
- What does cruciform love look like for you in this season?
- What does it look like to live formed and shaped like a cross at this particular moment?

I once asked a pastor just that—what does it look like to live cruciform right now—and I thought he would talk about *living surrendered.* I thought he would talk about *living given.* I thought he would say something practical, something I rather expected.

Instead he said: *"Love that's truly cruciform lives vulnerably open enough that your heart could know hurt."*

My breath kinda caught. To be clear, he wasn't speaking of anything in any abusive, toxic, masochistic kind of way—but he was speaking of a cruciform love that is deeply vulnerable. As C. S. Lewis writes, "To love at all is to be vulnerable. Love anything, and your heart will certainly be wrung and possibly be broken."[1]

Cruciform love bares its vulnerable heart—*and willingly bears the cost.*

Cruciform love isn't afraid of pain—*because it trusts there's more to gain.*

When we think of Jesus and cruciform faith, we often think of His crucifixion. Yet before He gave His life on the cross, He lived a life of daily deaths and resurrections—of noes to His plans and yeses to God's will—to bring life to others. He gave of Himself to bring good news to the poor and release for the captive, providing a way for those who've lost their way, for those whose hope has decayed. His heart turned toward those who were like lost sheep, lost children. On His way, *He stopped to heal the hurting because His cruciform heart goes toward others.*

The way forward is always toward others.

Cruciform love lives into the joy of *living given* in all things. Christ's way of givenness for the sake of others, showing the worth and chosenness of others, is living in the way He died, the way that led Him to rise: living the way of the cross.

There's more than believing Christ died for us—there's seeing that He practiced living this surrendered, given cross-shaped love in a thousand ways. And now He invites us into His sacred way of being, because every exodus, every way through, embraces the shape of the cross. Jesus invites us to be shaped by the wholly holy givenness of the cross, which leads to transformation—*because this is the gospel mission.* Jesus embodied this way of living most profoundly as He gave His life for humanity. Hands and feet nailed to the beams, arms outstretched in the tension of this world, He surrendered His will to His Father's, His heart turned toward loving others. Even as He was dying, Jesus showed this cruciform way of living—showing us the only way through this world, out of bondage, and into freedom.

Nothing formed against you can stand when you live cruciform, because cruciform is the form of surrender—and as you let yourself be formed cruciform, you let go of all that has been formed against you. Let yourself be formed cruciform: Open up your arms and heart into the posture of surrender, and let go.

Let go of any anxiousness about the unknown, about the future, about tomorrow. Let go of the overproductivity, the overactivity, the overwhelm. Let go of the failure, flailing, and fear over the future. Let go of the performance and the perfectionism and the pressure to impress. Let go of the worry and the hurry and the unhealthy addictions to needing approval. Let go of the heavy and hard and all the hopes that hurt deep.

Let go of all the what-ifs—and let the love of Jesus meet you now with the assurance that you are always safe and held, *even if the ways of God don't come to you the way you expected.*

How does it feel to see Jesus right now with His arms outstretched toward you?

Jesus' posture of cruciformity is receiving everything you are letting go of. Let Jesus, with His open arms, take it all.

And as you open up your arms and let it go—so Jesus can take it all, carry it all for you—let Jesus' open arms take you, let Jesus' open arms hold you, let Jesus' love carry you through. Simply let God lead you onward, let God love you now, let God make the way, let God's mind be your mind, let God's Word be your heart, let God's way be your way. Life is letting go: letting go of plans, and dreams, and maps, and expectations, and hopes, and vision, and brokenness. Let go—and let God take it all.

As tender as it is: You always have to keep on letting go of where you are. This is true: The very act of being a follower of Jesus is to be a surrenderer; *you can't keep following Him if you don't actually let go of where you are right now.*

What is King Jesus calling you to let go of today?

The only way through is to let go of the way you've come.

Surrender. Surrender to love. Even, especially, here. Let go—let Him love you any way He wants to love you. He is working His love into every single part of our story, because Love is who He is. This letting go, this living cruciform, can feel like we are sacrificing in deeply painful ways. Yet the Hebrew word for sacrifice means something very different. Sacrifice in Hebrew is *korban*, which literally means an approach, a moving closer. Sacrifice is not losing something *but moving closer to Someone.* Sacrifice isn't about loss; *sacrifice is about love.* Sacrifice isn't only about letting go—but about getting to move closer.

Sacrifice is about letting go of all that is in the way—so you get to draw nearer to what matters most. Sacrifice is about detaching from one thing—to attach to a greater thing.

Whenever we let go—we get to love more. When we live cruciform— we are formed into closer connections. *Cruciform is about being formed into love.*

Surrender to love.

- Putting pen to paper as prayer: How might you let go of something—give more of yourself to Him?
- How might you let go of one thing you're holding on to—and come even nearer to Love Himself?

Stretching out arms, palms turned wide open to the heavens in a posture of cruciformity, just let your heart pray honestly, offering your whole heart, your whole life to Him:

> *Here, Lord Jesus.*
> *Here are my paper-thin dreams.*
> *Here are my bruised and broken hopes.*
> *Here is my tattered map of the way I thought things would be.*
> *Here, take all my ways as my sacrifice laid down at Your feet.*
> *So now, please, just take me—so we can be close, near, here, right here.*

When you pray a *korban* prayer—a cruciform prayer of sacrifice and surrender—and you let go of more, you get to love more.

This is how you choose what you really want most: Let go of anything that is getting in the way, between you and the One who is the Way Himself.

The God who tenderly shaped you in your mother's womb, who gently shaped your life in the palm of His hand, He's shaped you to be cruciform, and you are in the best and most glorious shape of your life when you are shaped cruciform.

What might it look like today to love cruciform?

stillness to know God

How can I slow, still, and breathe in a place of trust with God today? (Psalm 46:10)
Still all the worry.... Hush all the hurry.... Breathe ... breathe deeply....
I live in the spacious, non-anxious presence of God.

_____

attentiveness to hear God

Who do I say that God is today? (Mark 8:29)

_____

_____

_____

Where am I coming from and where am I going to today? (Genesis 16:8)

_____

_____

_____

What do I want today? (John 1:38)

_____

_____

_____

cruciformity to surrender to God

What do I need to do or surrender to live cruciform today? (Luke 9:23)

_____

_____

_____

revelation to see God

How did I experience a fresh revelation from God in His Word today?
(Psalm 119:105)

_____

_____

_____

_____

_____

examine to return to God

What am I afraid of today? (Mark 4:40)

_____

_____

_____

_____

doxology to thank God

What can I thank God for today? (1 Thessalonians 5:18)

_____

_____

_____

What's God inviting me to do today, to make today a day of more
amazing grace?

_____

_____

stillness to know God

How can I slow, still, and breathe in a place of trust with God today?
(Psalm 46:10)
Still all the worry.... Hush all the hurry.... Breathe ... breathe deeply....
I live in the spacious, non-anxious presence of God.

_____

attentiveness to hear God

Who do I say that God is today? (Mark 8:29)

_____

_____

_____

Where am I coming from and where am I going to today? (Genesis 16:8)

_____

_____

_____

What do I want today? (John 1:38)

_____

_____

_____

cruciformity to surrender to God

What do I need to do or surrender to live cruciform today? (Luke 9:23)

_____

_____

_____

revelation to see God

How did I experience a fresh revelation from God in His Word today?
(Psalm 119:105)

_____

_____

_____

_____

_____

examine to return to God

What am I afraid of today? (Mark 4:40)

_____

_____

_____

_____

_____

doxology to thank God

What can I thank God for today? (1 Thessalonians 5:18)

_____

_____

_____

What's God inviting me to do today, to make today a day of more
amazing grace?

_____

_____

stillness to know God

How can I slow, still, and breathe in a place of trust with God today?
(Psalm 46:10)
Still all the worry.... Hush all the hurry.... Breathe ... breathe deeply....
I live in the spacious, non-anxious presence of God.

_____

attentiveness to hear God

Who do I say that God is today? (Mark 8:29)

_____

_____

_____

Where am I coming from and where am I going to today? (Genesis 16:8)

_____

_____

_____

What do I want today? (John 1:38)

_____

_____

_____

cruciformity to surrender to God

What do I need to do or surrender to live cruciform today? (Luke 9:23)

_____

_____

_____

revelation to see God

How did I experience a fresh revelation from God in His Word today? (Psalm 119:105)

_____

_____

_____

_____

_____

examine to return to God

What am I afraid of today? (Mark 4:40)

_____

_____

_____

_____

doxology to thank God

What can I thank God for today? (1 Thessalonians 5:18)

_____

_____

_____

What's God inviting me to do today, to make today a day of more amazing grace?

_____

_____

stillness to know God

How can I slow, still, and breathe in a place of trust with God today?
(Psalm 46:10)
Still all the worry. . . . Hush all the hurry. . . . Breathe . . . breathe deeply. . . .
I live in the spacious, non-anxious presence of God.

_____

attentiveness to hear God

Who do I say that God is today? (Mark 8:29)

_____

_____

_____

Where am I coming from and where am I going to today? (Genesis 16:8)

_____

_____

_____

What do I want today? (John 1:38)

_____

_____

_____

cruciformity to surrender to God

What do I need to do or surrender to live cruciform today? (Luke 9:23)

_____

_____

_____

revelation to see God

How did I experience a fresh revelation from God in His Word today?
(Psalm 119:105)

_____

_____

_____

_____

_____

examine to return to God

What am I afraid of today? (Mark 4:40)

_____

_____

_____

_____

_____

doxology to thank God

What can I thank God for today? (1 Thessalonians 5:18)

_____

_____

_____

What's God inviting me to do today, to make today a day of more
amazing grace?

_____

_____

stillness to know God

How can I slow, still, and breathe in a place of trust with God today?
(Psalm 46:10)
Still all the worry.... Hush all the hurry.... Breathe ... breathe deeply....
I live in the spacious, non-anxious presence of God.

_____

attentiveness to hear God

Who do I say that God is today? (Mark 8:29)

_____

_____

_____

Where am I coming from and where am I going to today? (Genesis 16:8)

_____

_____

_____

What do I want today? (John 1:38)

_____

_____

_____

cruciformity to surrender to God

What do I need to do or surrender to live cruciform today? (Luke 9:23)

_____

_____

_____

revelation to see God

How did I experience a fresh revelation from God in His Word today?
(Psalm 119:105)

_____

_____

_____

_____

_____

examine to return to God

What am I afraid of today? (Mark 4:40)

_____

_____

_____

_____

_____

doxology to thank God

What can I thank God for today? (1 Thessalonians 5:18)

_____

_____

_____

What's God inviting me to do today, to make today a day of more
amazing grace?

_____

_____

stillness to know God

How can I slow, still, and breathe in a place of trust with God today? (Psalm 46:10)

Still all the worry.... Hush all the hurry.... Breathe ... breathe deeply.... I live in the spacious, non-anxious presence of God.

_____

attentiveness to hear God

Who do I say that God is today? (Mark 8:29)

_____

_____

Where am I coming from and where am I going to today? (Genesis 16:8)

_____

_____

What do I want today? (John 1:38)

_____

_____

cruciformity to surrender to God

What do I need to do or surrender to live cruciform today? (Luke 9:23)

_____

_____

revelation to see God

How did I experience a fresh revelation from God in His Word today?
(Psalm 119:105)

_____

_____

_____

_____

_____

examine to return to God

What am I afraid of today? (Mark 4:40)

_____

_____

_____

_____

_____

doxology to thank God

What can I thank God for today? (1 Thessalonians 5:18)

_____

_____

_____

What's God inviting me to do today, to make today a day of more
amazing grace?

_____

_____

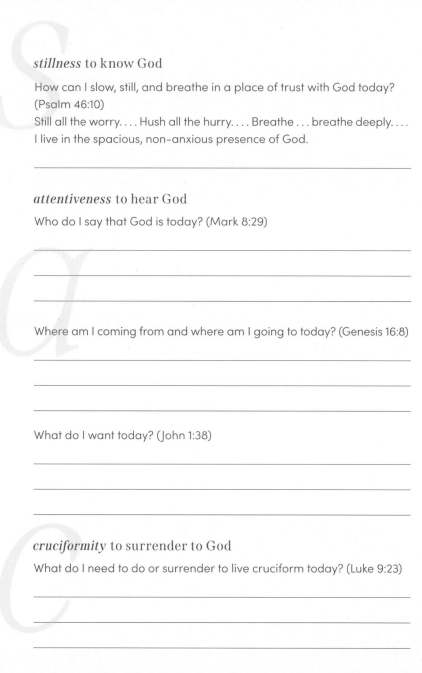

stillness to know God

How can I slow, still, and breathe in a place of trust with God today? (Psalm 46:10)
Still all the worry. . . . Hush all the hurry. . . . Breathe . . . breathe deeply. . . .
I live in the spacious, non-anxious presence of God.

_____

attentiveness to hear God

Who do I say that God is today? (Mark 8:29)

_____

_____

Where am I coming from and where am I going to today? (Genesis 16:8)

_____

_____

What do I want today? (John 1:38)

_____

_____

cruciformity to surrender to God

What do I need to do or surrender to live cruciform today? (Luke 9:23)

_____

_____

_____

revelation to see God

How did I experience a fresh revelation from God in His Word today?
(Psalm 119:105)

_____

_____

_____

_____

_____

examine to return to God

What am I afraid of today? (Mark 4:40)

_____

_____

_____

_____

_____

doxology to thank God

What can I thank God for today? (1 Thessalonians 5:18)

_____

_____

_____

What's God inviting me to do today, to make today a day of more
amazing grace?

_____

_____

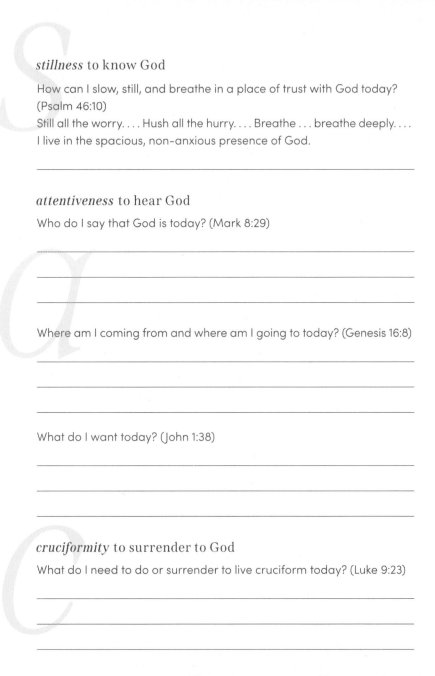

stillness to know God

How can I slow, still, and breathe in a place of trust with God today? (Psalm 46:10)
Still all the worry. . . . Hush all the hurry. . . . Breathe . . . breathe deeply. . . .
I live in the spacious, non-anxious presence of God.

_____

attentiveness to hear God

Who do I say that God is today? (Mark 8:29)

_____

_____

_____

Where am I coming from and where am I going to today? (Genesis 16:8)

_____

_____

_____

What do I want today? (John 1:38)

_____

_____

_____

cruciformity to surrender to God

What do I need to do or surrender to live cruciform today? (Luke 9:23)

_____

_____

_____

revelation to see God

How did I experience a fresh revelation from God in His Word today?
(Psalm 119:105)

_____

_____

_____

_____

_____

examine to return to God

What am I afraid of today? (Mark 4:40)

_____

_____

_____

_____

_____

doxology to thank God

What can I thank God for today? (1 Thessalonians 5:18)

_____

_____

_____

What's God inviting me to do today, to make today a day of more
amazing grace?

_____

_____

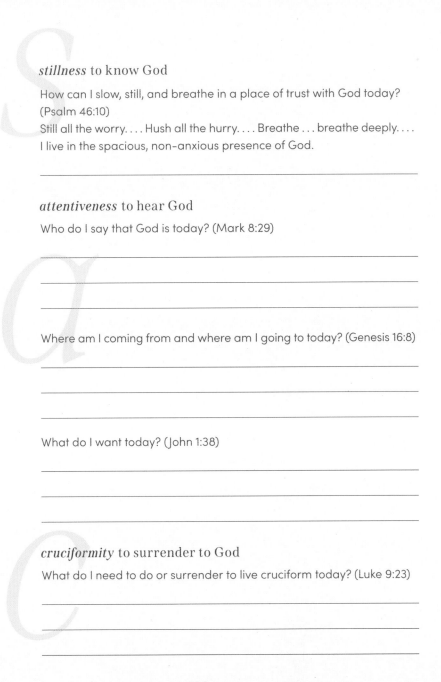

stillness to know God

How can I slow, still, and breathe in a place of trust with God today?
(Psalm 46:10)
Still all the worry.... Hush all the hurry.... Breathe ... breathe deeply....
I live in the spacious, non-anxious presence of God.

_____

attentiveness to hear God

Who do I say that God is today? (Mark 8:29)

_____

_____

_____

Where am I coming from and where am I going to today? (Genesis 16:8)

_____

_____

_____

What do I want today? (John 1:38)

_____

_____

_____

cruciformity to surrender to God

What do I need to do or surrender to live cruciform today? (Luke 9:23)

_____

_____

_____

revelation to see God

How did I experience a fresh revelation from God in His Word today?
(Psalm 119:105)

_____

_____

_____

_____

_____

examine to return to God

What am I afraid of today? (Mark 4:40)

_____

_____

_____

_____

doxology to thank God

What can I thank God for today? (1 Thessalonians 5:18)

_____

_____

_____

What's God inviting me to do today, to make today a day of more
amazing grace?

_____

_____

stillness to know God

How can I slow, still, and breathe in a place of trust with God today? (Psalm 46:10)
Still all the worry. . . . Hush all the hurry. . . . Breathe . . . breathe deeply. . . .
I live in the spacious, non-anxious presence of God.

_____

attentiveness to hear God

Who do I say that God is today? (Mark 8:29)

_____

_____

_____

Where am I coming from and where am I going to today? (Genesis 16:8)

_____

_____

_____

What do I want today? (John 1:38)

_____

_____

_____

cruciformity to surrender to God

What do I need to do or surrender to live cruciform today? (Luke 9:23)

_____

_____

_____

revelation to see God

How did I experience a fresh revelation from God in His Word today? (Psalm 119:105)

_____

_____

_____

_____

_____

examine to return to God

What am I afraid of today? (Mark 4:40)

_____

_____

_____

_____

doxology to thank God

What can I thank God for today? (1 Thessalonians 5:18)

_____

_____

_____

What's God inviting me to do today, to make today a day of more amazing grace?

_____

_____

stillness to know God

How can I slow, still, and breathe in a place of trust with God today?
(Psalm 46:10)
Still all the worry.... Hush all the hurry.... Breathe ... breathe deeply....
I live in the spacious, non-anxious presence of God.

_____

attentiveness to hear God

Who do I say that God is today? (Mark 8:29)

_____

_____

_____

Where am I coming from and where am I going to today? (Genesis 16:8)

_____

_____

_____

What do I want today? (John 1:38)

_____

_____

_____

cruciformity to surrender to God

What do I need to do or surrender to live cruciform today? (Luke 9:23)

_____

_____

_____

revelation to see God

How did I experience a fresh revelation from God in His Word today?
(Psalm 119:105)

_____

_____

_____

_____

_____

examine to return to God

What am I afraid of today? (Mark 4:40)

_____

_____

_____

_____

doxology to thank God

What can I thank God for today? (1 Thessalonians 5:18)

_____

_____

_____

What's God inviting me to do today, to make today a day of more
amazing grace?

_____

_____

stillness to know God

How can I slow, still, and breathe in a place of trust with God today?
(Psalm 46:10)
Still all the worry.... Hush all the hurry.... Breathe ... breathe deeply....
I live in the spacious, non-anxious presence of God.

_____

attentiveness to hear God

Who do I say that God is today? (Mark 8:29)

_____

_____

_____

Where am I coming from and where am I going to today? (Genesis 16:8)

_____

_____

_____

What do I want today? (John 1:38)

_____

_____

_____

cruciformity to surrender to God

What do I need to do or surrender to live cruciform today? (Luke 9:23)

_____

_____

_____

revelation to see God

How did I experience a fresh revelation from God in His Word today?
(Psalm 119:105)

_____

_____

_____

_____

_____

examine to return to God

What am I afraid of today? (Mark 4:40)

_____

_____

_____

_____

doxology to thank God

What can I thank God for today? (1 Thessalonians 5:18)

_____

_____

_____

What's God inviting me to do today, to make today a day of more
amazing grace?

_____

_____

stillness to know God

How can I slow, still, and breathe in a place of trust with God today?
(Psalm 46:10)
Still all the worry.... Hush all the hurry.... Breathe ... breathe deeply....
I live in the spacious, non-anxious presence of God.

_____

attentiveness to hear God

Who do I say that God is today? (Mark 8:29)

_____

_____

_____

Where am I coming from and where am I going to today? (Genesis 16:8)

_____

_____

_____

What do I want today? (John 1:38)

_____

_____

_____

cruciformity to surrender to God

What do I need to do or surrender to live cruciform today? (Luke 9:23)

_____

_____

_____

revelation to see God

How did I experience a fresh revelation from God in His Word today? (Psalm 119:105)

_____

_____

_____

_____

_____

examine to return to God

What am I afraid of today? (Mark 4:40)

_____

_____

_____

_____

_____

doxology to thank God

What can I thank God for today? (1 Thessalonians 5:18)

_____

_____

_____

What's God inviting me to do today, to make today a day of more amazing grace?

_____

_____

stillness to know God

How can I slow, still, and breathe in a place of trust with God today? (Psalm 46:10)
Still all the worry.... Hush all the hurry.... Breathe ... breathe deeply....
I live in the spacious, non-anxious presence of God.

_____

attentiveness to hear God

Who do I say that God is today? (Mark 8:29)

_____

_____

_____

Where am I coming from and where am I going to today? (Genesis 16:8)

_____

_____

_____

What do I want today? (John 1:38)

_____

_____

_____

cruciformity to surrender to God

What do I need to do or surrender to live cruciform today? (Luke 9:23)

_____

_____

_____

revelation to see God

How did I experience a fresh revelation from God in His Word today?
(Psalm 119:105)

_____

_____

_____

_____

_____

examine to return to God

What am I afraid of today? (Mark 4:40)

_____

_____

_____

_____

_____

doxology to thank God

What can I thank God for today? (1 Thessalonians 5:18)

_____

_____

_____

What's God inviting me to do today, to make today a day of more
amazing grace?

_____

_____

stillness to know God

How can I slow, still, and breathe in a place of trust with God today?
(Psalm 46:10)
Still all the worry.... Hush all the hurry.... Breathe ... breathe deeply....
I live in the spacious, non-anxious presence of God.

_____

attentiveness to hear God

Who do I say that God is today? (Mark 8:29)

_____

_____

_____

Where am I coming from and where am I going to today? (Genesis 16:8)

_____

_____

_____

What do I want today? (John 1:38)

_____

_____

_____

cruciformity to surrender to God

What do I need to do or surrender to live cruciform today? (Luke 9:23)

_____

_____

_____

revelation to see God

How did I experience a fresh revelation from God in His Word today? (Psalm 119:105)

_____

_____

_____

_____

_____

examine to return to God

What am I afraid of today? (Mark 4:40)

_____

_____

_____

_____

_____

doxology to thank God

What can I thank God for today? (1 Thessalonians 5:18)

_____

_____

_____

What's God inviting me to do today, to make today a day of more amazing grace?

_____

_____

This is why we read the Word: We don't read the Word to merely know how to obey God's will for us; we read the Word to know God, to have a fresh revelation of God, and to understand how He is for us.

The Word of God is not meant to be read merely for some personal revelation, to answer some question; it is meant to be read for a revelation of God's heart so we choose a deeper relationship with Him.

Ultimately: *The Word is read for a revelation of Love, who came for relationship.* You read the page, the Word, to fall in love with a Person, the Word.

Because: There is a knowing that is only information, and there is a knowing that is holy intimacy. There is a knownness of intellectual acknowledgment, and there is an intimate knownness of deep affection. The sacred call is to know God—in Hebrew, to *yada* God. *Yada* is a Hebrew action of knowing that denotes "concern, inner engagement, dedication, or attachment to a person."[1] There is a knowing that is surface-level, and *there is a knowing that is intimate, soul to soul.*

This is the sacred way of Jesus: more than only information or instruction, always, ultimately intimacy. A sacred, intimate knowing is the only real knowing of God.

The power to change a life is in His Word. Stay in the Word, and your soul will be moved: moved in the only direction that matters, that heals, that fulfills, that steadies, that comforts, that revives you. Every line of God's Word is like an axle—turning the soul around, moving the soul forward.

Getting you there. *Getting you into the arms of God.* What if we kept turning our direction so that God is always our destination?

The goal isn't ever a place; the goal is always a Person. The goal is the presence of your Provider, your peace, your purpose, your Person . . . *your Jesus.*

The goal isn't to walk somewhere; it is to walk with Someone.

God is the goal.

There is only One who can intercept what's coming after you and keep you alive. There is only One who can keep the fears and worries hunting you down at bay.

God's Word is a living Spirit-book, and the Spirit Himself speaks through the every page of God's Word, a certain revelation of God and His heart. And every time we read from God's Word, when we see a fresh revelation of God and who He is in His Word, this is nothing short of apocalyptic—which is what revelation literally means: *apokalupsis*!

There is never a revelation of God without an apocalypse in us. Every revelation from God is a cataclysmic deconstruction of our kingdom, rebuilding us into more of God's kingdom.

What Are We Building?

Apparently, every minute, more than one half of us—over four billion people on this planet—are liking a Facebook post.

During our average twelve waking hours—twenty-three words grab for our attention every single second. Twenty-three words per second through our phones, email, TVs, radio, newspapers.

How many of them are His Words? If a life is built on hustling work instead of the holy Word, built on social media instead of Scripture meditation, built on the pursuit of comfort instead of prayer and the comfort of the

Holy Spirit, then a life cannot stand—and eventually nothing of any eternal good will be left standing.

Apathy for His Word leads to atrophy of a soul. It is tender to sit with the reality: Only our own lack of love can keep us from His love letter. Only being captivated by other words can keep us from His Word. It's never that we don't have enough time; it's always that we have different priorities.

The enemy plots our destruction through distraction—distraction from God's Word, God's voice, God's ways, God's revelation. Give up distractions to keep your soul from destruction. And there is always a way to shave minutes off here, carve out more there, trim a few there, pare a bit here— then gather up the holy moments and make sacred time for what you want. Time is made for what we love.

Wherever love and priorities meet, time is made. We always make time for what we love. For whom we love. Giving up something for the love of Jesus isn't really giving up anything—when He gave up everything for the ones He loves.

There's a giving up that only gains. There's an offering that only fulfills. There's a sacrifice that is no sacrifice at all. Your loves alone limit how much of God you have.

Your wants, your habits, your priorities, and your choices limit how much of God you have.

You can have as much of God—of His hope, of His courage, of His love, of a fresh revelation of God in His Word—as you actually want.

And it's a quieting, healing truth: Reading His Word is not about getting Him to love you, but about getting yourself to the place where you can hear Him tell you He loves you.

Only drinking from His well of words can satisfy. God's Word is not only an early-morning book, or a compartmentalized book, or a "quiet time" book, but an anytime-everywhere book that is always your secure base, that is always the most exquisite elixir for the soul.

For as the well of God's Word says: Streams of life-giving water will fill and brim and overflow from anyone who comes to Him when overwhelmed (John 7:37–38, paraphrased). If you are thirsty, go not to the tap of distraction, or to the immediate gratification fridge, or out to the water well of modern escapism, where you keep swallowing it down but never feel well—but come, come to the Word and well and beauty of Jesus and drink deep and long, to the soul's deep quenching content and delight.

Where there's no seeking a fresh revelation of God, but a hoarding of old manna gathered from yesterdays in the company of God, we can count on that manna to grow stale and rot and nauseate our one and only life.

The deepest truth is: You are not alone, and life is hard not because you've done something wrong, but because you are human and being human is hard in a world of wrongs. When we stay in the living, spirit-filled Word, we read the revelatory truth about our Father's world that touches every tribulation and heartbreak we have ever known: "Our present sufferings are not worth comparing with the glory that will be revealed in us" (Romans 8:18 NIV).

> Not only that, but we rejoice in our sufferings, knowing that suffering produces endurance, and endurance produces character, and character produces hope, and hope does not put us to shame, because God's love has been poured into our hearts through the Holy Spirit who has been given to us (Romans 5:3–5 ESV).

God's Word reveals that your suffering isn't a waste, isn't for nothing. Your suffering actually produces something; your suffering produces good endurance, which produces good character, and that good character produces great hope. Suffering is never for nothing, but is being worked into the most meaningful, eternal, good things.

Yet this can be hard to see, to know, to understand without this continuous habit of soul, which returns to the Word for a revelation of the realest reality.

Without the lens of the Word, the world warps.

But with the Word? "Everything's falling apart on me, GOD; put me together again with your Word" (Psalm 119:107 MSG).

Steep in it, meditate on it, return to it, carry a verse of it, and don't begin the day without it. Don't try to face the day until you've sought the face of God. Unless we reach for our first love, the Word Himself, first thing, nothing's going to turn out in the end. Only when we have a fresh revelation of God every day can we have a certain direction for our day. So that's the holy invitation: *Get into God's Word and let it get into you.* Before the day overwhelms you, come close and feel His love over everything. Start in that place, the place where you open His Word and hear Him tell you He loves you. Let His love words shape your world today. Because it's true every single morning, time and again, and it never stops being the revelation our heart yearns for: *We don't read His Word to get God's love; we read it to get in a place where we can feel God's love for us again.*

"Take to heart all the words I have solemnly declared to you . . . *they are your life*" (Deuteronomy 32:46–47 NIV, emphasis added). His Word to us is never a passing word or line—His Word is our very lifeline. Like Jonathan Edwards said, our God is a communicative being. And there is nothing like knowing that the communicative God wants to communicate with you. Our God is a communicative being who never stops communicating truth to a world that is in a brutal communication war to decide truth. In tumultuous times, only one voice can calm seas . . . and to neglect the only voice that calms waves is to invite internal chaos. One day, either this world will blow apart, or our own world will blow apart—and the only way we're going to survive is if we've set time apart to let God's revelatory Spirit blow in.

- Putting pen to paper as prayer in reflection, in confession, in communion: In what ways might your life, your days, your moments look like you want a clear revelation from God more than you want a close relationship with God?
- How are you daily inviting the Word of God into your heart?
- In what ways might you be giving lip service to the Word of God—but in other ways not giving your life in service to God?

The sacred Spirit book of God is a telescope; look through it, and you have a revelation of the heart of God and all that is beyond imagination.

But if you only look *at* the Word of God, everything is flattened. The Spirit-filled book of God is meant to be gazed through—for a fresh revelation of God, of His love for you, of reality, of truth, so you might be transformed from within.

No matter where we are on the way, it turns out: *Turn the pages of His Word, and your life can turn around.* Put one foot in front of the other, and you can have another life. We can turn from the narrative of self and walk into the narrative of grace. The relief of this is everything. We can turn off all the noise of news and drama and distractions around us, and all the noise of fear and failure within us, and we can lean into the language of God.

God is the steady, consistent voice of love who tells us how to take the next step and the next step after that. If we let our feet literally keep rhythm with the Word of God, fears can stop driving our life. When we are spiritually moved by His Word, thoughts begin to move through our minds differently, and we begin to move through the world differently. As the Proverb says, "Where there is no revelation, people cast off restraint; but blessed is the one who heeds wisdom's instruction" (Proverbs 29:18 NIV). If we stay in the Word of God, our life stays on course, with the Way Himself, through the confusion and heartache of this world, and when we get in the Word and get the Word in us, we realize: We survived 100 percent of our worst days—and God will reveal a sacred way for us to move through every day when we let Him and His Word move us. "Beloved, now we are children of God; and it has not yet been revealed what we shall be, but we know that when He is revealed, we shall be like Him, for we shall see Him as He is" (1 John 3:2 NKJV). We don't have to keep up with anyone else; we're simply invited to keep company with God—*the only One who has ever loved us to death and back to the realest life.*

These times need us: Who will be steadfast stewards of the sacred story of God if not us?

Genuine restoration only happens when people seek a fresh, sacred revelation of God—when people seek the only story that can shelter generations with any real hope of regeneration, transformative salvation, and daily direction.

When His Word begins to dwell in you, you come home to rest.

So now is the moment your soul can whisper in this sacred space,

I will delight in Your commandments,
  Which I love.
  And I shall lift up my hands to Your commandments,
  Which I love;
  And I will meditate on Your statutes (Psalm 119:47–48 NASB).

Here is your sacred prayer.

stillness to know God

How can I slow, still, and breathe in a place of trust with God today?
(Psalm 46:10)
Still all the worry.... Hush all the hurry.... Breathe ... breathe deeply....
I live in the spacious, non-anxious presence of God.

_____

attentiveness to hear God

Who do I say that God is today? (Mark 8:29)

_____

_____

_____

Where am I coming from and where am I going to today? (Genesis 16:8)

_____

_____

_____

What do I want today? (John 1:38)

_____

_____

_____

cruciformity to surrender to God

What do I need to do or surrender to live cruciform today? (Luke 9:23)

_____

_____

_____

revelation to see God

How did I experience a fresh revelation from God in His Word today?
(Psalm 119:105)

_____

_____

_____

_____

_____

examine to return to God

What am I afraid of today? (Mark 4:40)

_____

_____

_____

_____

_____

doxology to thank God

What can I thank God for today? (1 Thessalonians 5:18)

_____

_____

_____

What's God inviting me to do today, to make today a day of more
amazing grace?

_____

_____

stillness to know God

How can I slow, still, and breathe in a place of trust with God today?
(Psalm 46:10)
Still all the worry. . . . Hush all the hurry. . . . Breathe . . . breathe deeply. . . .
I live in the spacious, non-anxious presence of God.

_____

attentiveness to hear God

Who do I say that God is today? (Mark 8:29)

_____

_____

_____

Where am I coming from and where am I going to today? (Genesis 16:8)

_____

_____

_____

What do I want today? (John 1:38)

_____

_____

_____

cruciformity to surrender to God

What do I need to do or surrender to live cruciform today? (Luke 9:23)

_____

_____

_____

revelation to see God

How did I experience a fresh revelation from God in His Word today? (Psalm 119:105)

_____

_____

_____

_____

_____

examine to return to God

What am I afraid of today? (Mark 4:40)

_____

_____

_____

_____

_____

doxology to thank God

What can I thank God for today? (1 Thessalonians 5:18)

_____

_____

_____

What's God inviting me to do today, to make today a day of more amazing grace?

_____

_____

stillness to know God

How can I slow, still, and breathe in a place of trust with God today? (Psalm 46:10)
Still all the worry. . . . Hush all the hurry. . . . Breathe . . . breathe deeply. . . .
I live in the spacious, non-anxious presence of God.

_____

attentiveness to hear God

Who do I say that God is today? (Mark 8:29)

_____

_____

_____

Where am I coming from and where am I going to today? (Genesis 16:8)

_____

_____

_____

What do I want today? (John 1:38)

_____

_____

_____

cruciformity to surrender to God

What do I need to do or surrender to live cruciform today? (Luke 9:23)

_____

_____

_____

revelation to see God

How did I experience a fresh revelation from God in His Word today?
(Psalm 119:105)

_____

_____

_____

_____

_____

examine to return to God

What am I afraid of today? (Mark 4:40)

_____

_____

_____

_____

_____

doxology to thank God

What can I thank God for today? (1 Thessalonians 5:18)

_____

_____

_____

What's God inviting me to do today, to make today a day of more
amazing grace?

_____

_____

stillness to know God

How can I slow, still, and breathe in a place of trust with God today?
(Psalm 46:10)
Still all the worry. . . . Hush all the hurry. . . . Breathe . . . breathe deeply. . . .
I live in the spacious, non-anxious presence of God.

_____

attentiveness to hear God

Who do I say that God is today? (Mark 8:29)

_____

_____

_____

Where am I coming from and where am I going to today? (Genesis 16:8)

_____

_____

_____

What do I want today? (John 1:38)

_____

_____

_____

cruciformity to surrender to God

What do I need to do or surrender to live cruciform today? (Luke 9:23)

_____

_____

_____

DAY 49

revelation to see God

How did I experience a fresh revelation from God in His Word today?
(Psalm 119:105)

_____

_____

_____

_____

_____

examine to return to God

What am I afraid of today? (Mark 4:40)

_____

_____

_____

_____

doxology to thank God

What can I thank God for today? (1 Thessalonians 5:18)

_____

_____

_____

What's God inviting me to do today, to make today a day of more
amazing grace?

_____

_____

stillness to know God

How can I slow, still, and breathe in a place of trust with God today?
(Psalm 46:10)
Still all the worry. . . . Hush all the hurry. . . . Breathe . . . breathe deeply. . . .
I live in the spacious, non-anxious presence of God.

_____

attentiveness to hear God

Who do I say that God is today? (Mark 8:29)

_____

_____

_____

Where am I coming from and where am I going to today? (Genesis 16:8)

_____

_____

_____

What do I want today? (John 1:38)

_____

_____

_____

cruciformity to surrender to God

What do I need to do or surrender to live cruciform today? (Luke 9:23)

_____

_____

_____

revelation to see God

How did I experience a fresh revelation from God in His Word today?
(Psalm 119:105)

_____

_____

_____

_____

_____

examine to return to God

What am I afraid of today? (Mark 4:40)

_____

_____

_____

_____

_____

doxology to thank God

What can I thank God for today? (1 Thessalonians 5:18)

_____

_____

_____

What's God inviting me to do today, to make today a day of more
amazing grace?

_____

_____

131

stillness to know God

How can I slow, still, and breathe in a place of trust with God today? (Psalm 46:10)
Still all the worry. . . . Hush all the hurry. . . . Breathe . . . breathe deeply. . . .
I live in the spacious, non-anxious presence of God.

_____

attentiveness to hear God

Who do I say that God is today? (Mark 8:29)

_____

_____

_____

Where am I coming from and where am I going to today? (Genesis 16:8)

_____

_____

_____

What do I want today? (John 1:38)

_____

_____

_____

cruciformity to surrender to God

What do I need to do or surrender to live cruciform today? (Luke 9:23)

_____

_____

_____

revelation to see God

How did I experience a fresh revelation from God in His Word today?
(Psalm 119:105)

_____

_____

_____

_____

_____

examine to return to God

What am I afraid of today? (Mark 4:40)

_____

_____

_____

_____

_____

doxology to thank God

What can I thank God for today? (1 Thessalonians 5:18)

_____

_____

_____

What's God inviting me to do today, to make today a day of more
amazing grace?

_____

_____

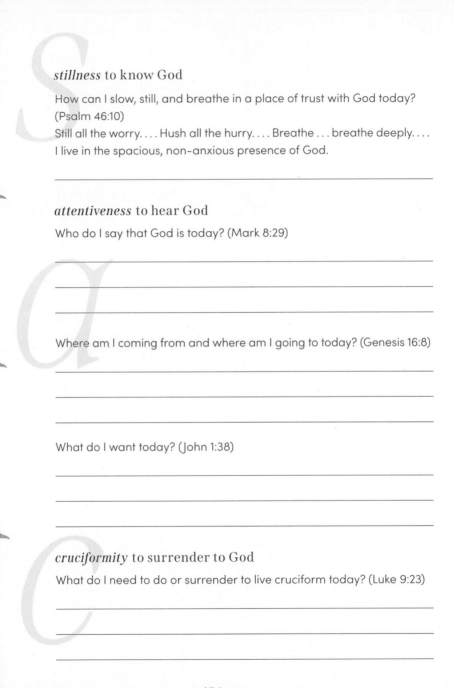

stillness to know God

How can I slow, still, and breathe in a place of trust with God today?
(Psalm 46:10)
Still all the worry. . . . Hush all the hurry. . . . Breathe . . . breathe deeply. . . .
I live in the spacious, non-anxious presence of God.

_____

attentiveness to hear God

Who do I say that God is today? (Mark 8:29)

_____

_____

_____

Where am I coming from and where am I going to today? (Genesis 16:8)

_____

_____

_____

What do I want today? (John 1:38)

_____

_____

_____

cruciformity to surrender to God

What do I need to do or surrender to live cruciform today? (Luke 9:23)

_____

_____

_____

revelation to see God

How did I experience a fresh revelation from God in His Word today? (Psalm 119:105)

_____

_____

_____

_____

_____

examine to return to God

What am I afraid of today? (Mark 4:40)

_____

_____

_____

_____

_____

doxology to thank God

What can I thank God for today? (1 Thessalonians 5:18)

_____

_____

_____

What's God inviting me to do today, to make today a day of more amazing grace?

_____

_____

stillness to know God

How can I slow, still, and breathe in a place of trust with God today?
(Psalm 46:10)
Still all the worry.... Hush all the hurry.... Breathe ... breathe deeply....
I live in the spacious, non-anxious presence of God.

_____

attentiveness to hear God

Who do I say that God is today? (Mark 8:29)

_____

_____

_____

Where am I coming from and where am I going to today? (Genesis 16:8)

_____

_____

_____

What do I want today? (John 1:38)

_____

_____

_____

cruciformity to surrender to God

What do I need to do or surrender to live cruciform today? (Luke 9:23)

_____

_____

_____

revelation to see God

How did I experience a fresh revelation from God in His Word today? (Psalm 119:105)

_____

_____

_____

_____

_____

examine to return to God

What am I afraid of today? (Mark 4:40)

_____

_____

_____

_____

_____

doxology to thank God

What can I thank God for today? (1 Thessalonians 5:18)

_____

_____

_____

What's God inviting me to do today, to make today a day of more amazing grace?

_____

_____

stillness to know God

How can I slow, still, and breathe in a place of trust with God today?
(Psalm 46:10)
Still all the worry.... Hush all the hurry.... Breathe ... breathe deeply....
I live in the spacious, non-anxious presence of God.

_____

attentiveness to hear God

Who do I say that God is today? (Mark 8:29)

_____

_____

_____

Where am I coming from and where am I going to today? (Genesis 16:8)

_____

_____

_____

What do I want today? (John 1:38)

_____

_____

_____

cruciformity to surrender to God

What do I need to do or surrender to live cruciform today? (Luke 9:23)

_____

_____

_____

DAY 54

revelation to see God

How did I experience a fresh revelation from God in His Word today?
(Psalm 119:105)

_____

_____

_____

_____

_____

examine to return to God

What am I afraid of today? (Mark 4:40)

_____

_____

_____

_____

_____

doxology to thank God

What can I thank God for today? (1 Thessalonians 5:18)

_____

_____

_____

What's God inviting me to do today, to make today a day of more
amazing grace?

_____

_____

stillness to know God

How can I slow, still, and breathe in a place of trust with God today? (Psalm 46:10)
Still all the worry. . . . Hush all the hurry. . . . Breathe . . . breathe deeply. . . .
I live in the spacious, non-anxious presence of God.

_____

attentiveness to hear God

Who do I say that God is today? (Mark 8:29)

_____

_____

_____

Where am I coming from and where am I going to today? (Genesis 16:8)

_____

_____

_____

What do I want today? (John 1:38)

_____

_____

_____

cruciformity to surrender to God

What do I need to do or surrender to live cruciform today? (Luke 9:23)

_____

_____

_____

revelation to see God

How did I experience a fresh revelation from God in His Word today?
(Psalm 119:105)

_____

_____

_____

_____

_____

examine to return to God

What am I afraid of today? (Mark 4:40)

_____

_____

_____

_____

_____

doxology to thank God

What can I thank God for today? (1 Thessalonians 5:18)

_____

_____

_____

What's God inviting me to do today, to make today a day of more
amazing grace?

_____

_____

stillness to know God

How can I slow, still, and breathe in a place of trust with God today?
(Psalm 46:10)
Still all the worry. . . . Hush all the hurry. . . . Breathe . . . breathe deeply. . . .
I live in the spacious, non-anxious presence of God.

_____

attentiveness to hear God

Who do I say that God is today? (Mark 8:29)

_____

_____

_____

Where am I coming from and where am I going to today? (Genesis 16:8)

_____

_____

_____

What do I want today? (John 1:38)

_____

_____

_____

cruciformity to surrender to God

What do I need to do or surrender to live cruciform today? (Luke 9:23)

_____

_____

_____

revelation to see God

How did I experience a fresh revelation from God in His Word today?
(Psalm 119:105)

_____

_____

_____

_____

_____

examine to return to God

What am I afraid of today? (Mark 4:40)

_____

_____

_____

_____

doxology to thank God

What can I thank God for today? (1 Thessalonians 5:18)

_____

_____

What's God inviting me to do today, to make today a day of more amazing grace?

_____

_____

stillness to know God

How can I slow, still, and breathe in a place of trust with God today? (Psalm 46:10)

Still all the worry.... Hush all the hurry.... Breathe ... breathe deeply....
I live in the spacious, non-anxious presence of God.

_____

attentiveness to hear God

Who do I say that God is today? (Mark 8:29)

_____

_____

_____

Where am I coming from and where am I going to today? (Genesis 16:8)

_____

_____

_____

What do I want today? (John 1:38)

_____

_____

_____

cruciformity to surrender to God

What do I need to do or surrender to live cruciform today? (Luke 9:23)

_____

_____

_____

revelation to see God

How did I experience a fresh revelation from God in His Word today?
(Psalm 119:105)

_____

_____

_____

_____

_____

examine to return to God

What am I afraid of today? (Mark 4:40)

_____

_____

_____

_____

_____

doxology to thank God

What can I thank God for today? (1 Thessalonians 5:18)

_____

_____

_____

What's God inviting me to do today, to make today a day of more
amazing grace?

_____

_____

stillness to know God

How can I slow, still, and breathe in a place of trust with God today?
(Psalm 46:10)
Still all the worry. . . . Hush all the hurry. . . . Breathe . . . breathe deeply. . . .
I live in the spacious, non-anxious presence of God.

_____

attentiveness to hear God

Who do I say that God is today? (Mark 8:29)

_____

_____

_____

Where am I coming from and where am I going to today? (Genesis 16:8)

_____

_____

_____

What do I want today? (John 1:38)

_____

_____

_____

cruciformity to surrender to God

What do I need to do or surrender to live cruciform today? (Luke 9:23)

_____

_____

_____

revelation to see God

How did I experience a fresh revelation from God in His Word today?
(Psalm 119:105)

_____

_____

_____

_____

_____

examine to return to God

What am I afraid of today? (Mark 4:40)

_____

_____

_____

_____

doxology to thank God

What can I thank God for today? (1 Thessalonians 5:18)

_____

_____

_____

What's God inviting me to do today, to make today a day of more
amazing grace?

_____

_____

stillness to know God

How can I slow, still, and breathe in a place of trust with God today?
(Psalm 46:10)
Still all the worry. . . . Hush all the hurry. . . . Breathe . . . breathe deeply. . . .
I live in the spacious, non-anxious presence of God.

_____

attentiveness to hear God

Who do I say that God is today? (Mark 8:29)

_____

_____

_____

Where am I coming from and where am I going to today? (Genesis 16:8)

_____

_____

_____

What do I want today? (John 1:38)

_____

_____

_____

cruciformity to surrender to God

What do I need to do or surrender to live cruciform today? (Luke 9:23)

_____

_____

_____

revelation to see God

How did I experience a fresh revelation from God in His Word today? (Psalm 119:105)

_____
_____
_____
_____
_____

examine to return to God

What am I afraid of today? (Mark 4:40)

_____
_____
_____
_____
_____

doxology to thank God

What can I thank God for today? (1 Thessalonians 5:18)

_____
_____
_____

What's God inviting me to do today, to make today a day of more amazing grace?

_____
_____

stillness to know God

How can I slow, still, and breathe in a place of trust with God today? (Psalm 46:10)
Still all the worry. . . . Hush all the hurry. . . . Breathe . . . breathe deeply. . . .
I live in the spacious, non-anxious presence of God.

_____

attentiveness to hear God

Who do I say that God is today? (Mark 8:29)

_____

_____

_____

Where am I coming from and where am I going to today? (Genesis 16:8)

_____

_____

_____

What do I want today? (John 1:38)

_____

_____

_____

cruciformity to surrender to God

What do I need to do or surrender to live cruciform today? (Luke 9:23)

_____

_____

_____

revelation to see God

How did I experience a fresh revelation from God in His Word today? (Psalm 119:105)

_____

_____

_____

_____

_____

examine to return to God

What am I afraid of today? (Mark 4:40)

_____

_____

_____

_____

_____

doxology to thank God

What can I thank God for today? (1 Thessalonians 5:18)

_____

_____

_____

What's God inviting me to do today, to make today a day of more amazing grace?

_____

_____

Examine

It's only the examined life that passes the tests of life. And any life unexamined ends up unfulfilling. The truth is: Passing your days with no soul examination is how you fail your only life.

Didn't David say, "I have considered my ways and have turned my steps to your statutes" (Psalm 119:59 NIV)—because God Himself said, "Consider your ways" (Haggai 1:5 ESV)? Didn't Paul implore: "Each one must examine his own work" (Galatians 6:4 NASB)? Didn't the Israelites have a sacred pause of reflection and examine after the exodus: "Thus the LORD saved Israel that day from the hand of the Egyptians, and Israel saw the Egyptians dead on the seashore. Israel saw the great power that the LORD used against the Egyptians, so the people feared the LORD, and they believed in the LORD and in his servant Moses" (Exodus 14:30–31 ESV)?

The children of Israel saw what God did that day; Israel saw the great power of God; Israel reflected on the work God had done; Israel examined how the hand of God had forged an impossible way. At the end of the day, Israel examined God's hand—and it changed their hearts.

Maybe when we have a sacred rhythm of reliving the day, we see more reasons to keep believing in the Lord. Maybe part of the way out of the hard is to examine our hearts. Maybe there's no exodus without an examine.

Maybe when we feel lost, like there is no way, we need to make a habit of examining the way we are actually going. Maybe here, in this sacred moment, the invitation is to whisper with God's people: "Let's examine and search out our ways, and let's return to the LORD" (Lamentations 3:40 NASB).

It can be easy to examine the ways of others, the news, the noise, the neighbors, or the streams of Instagram or Facebook, all so much easier than examining our own hearts. Because maybe what we are most fearful of is facing all of what we are feeling. *Fear of deeply feeling loss, of deeply feeling anger, of deeply feeling abandoned, rejected, disappointed, shamed, disliked, unwanted, unseen.*

It's tempting to become addicted to living fast and furious, addicted to screens and work and whirl and noise and distractions because we are afraid of being still long enough to examine our own hearts, to feel what's in our hearts . . . and to let what we really feel and fear catch up to us, to let ourselves come face-to-face with a very real, intimate God who came to hold and mend the hurting places. You can spend a lifetime trying to outpace the pain, but when you still long enough to examine your feelings and hold space for the pain, you can feel the pain finally releasing its hold on you.

David was a man after God's own heart, a shepherd and king, our Old Testament shadow of the glorious Messiah, King Jesus. For a time, though, David did not examine what was in his own heart, did not examine his own fear of not being loved enough, did not examine his fear of not being wanted enough. Instead, David examined what was out his window, examined who was out bathing next door. *Bathsheba.* When we only examine the ways of everyone around us, instead of examining the ways that are actually within us, we can expect our hearts to eventually go wayward.

If we don't examine the ways our hearts turn, it can be our very lives that end up not turning out as we hoped.

David withdrew from his responsibilities and drew close to what he thought would comfort him, satisfy him, fulfill him. Living an unexamined life can end up exploding your life.

David wrote: "When I kept silent, my bones wasted away through my groaning all day long. For day and night your hand was heavy on me; my strength was sapped as in the heat of summer. Then I acknowledged my sin to you and did not cover up my iniquity. I said, 'I will confess my transgressions to the LORD.' And you forgave the guilt of my sin" (Psalm 32:3–5 NIV).

When David examined what was within him, He began to be changed from within. Vulnerably, he wrote in Psalm 51 of his own heart examination:

- You desire truth in the innermost being, and in secret You will make wisdom known to me. Purify me with hyssop, and I will be clean; cleanse me, and I will be whiter than snow (Psalm 51:6–7 NASB).
- Create in me a pure heart, O God, and renew a steadfast spirit within me. Do not cast me from your presence or take your Holy Spirit from me (Psalm 51:10–11).
- The sacrifices of God are a broken spirit; a broken and contrite heart, O God, you will not despise (Psalm 51:17 ESV).

Ultimately, our sacred prayer joins David's, and we experience the interior revolution: *We examine our hearts—to return our hearts to God.*

Return and repentance walk hand in hand, as the literal definition of repentance is to *turn* from sin in remorse—and every time we turn *from* something, we turn *to* something. As we turn from fears, from sin, from everything that lies and tells us it will comfort us more than God Himself, we turn our eyes upon the wide-open arms of Jesus—and return to God.

The thing always is: Before we can turn and return, we first must turn to examine the ways our hearts turn toward ourselves. We must examine all the ways fear makes us turn before we can let the love of Jesus turn us toward Love Himself. Jesus asks us to examine our hearts when He asks of His disciples, then and now, "Why are you so afraid?" (Mark 4:40 NIV). This is worth examining daily. Because: Behind much sin is often much fear.

Driving much darkness is much fearfulness. We may think we are driven by our wants, but too often we are driven by our fears. Only when you name and express your fears can the fears begin to ebb, which is why the Word asks us to calm our fears by putting words to them, by bringing them to the Word: "Do not be anxious about anything, but in every situation, by prayer and petition, with thanksgiving, present your requests to God. And the peace of God, which transcends all understanding, will guard your hearts and your minds in Christ Jesus" (Philippians 4:6–7 NIV).

Putting pen to paper as prayer, examining feelings and fears and communicating them to our Father, this is needful, sacred work because: Communication of feelings brings regulation to feelings. Only what you name can you regulate. *Emotion* literally means to move. Emotions are meant to move us toward each other and God, to move us to vulnerably share. Sharing our fears with our Father regulates our fears. Sharing the weight of fears and feelings with another soul, with God on these sacred pages, regulates a whole range of feelings, bringing deep balance and equilibrium to our souls.

Jesus asks us to examine why we are so afraid because He knows: our fears masquerade like anger, like control, like perfectionism, like procrastination, like self-harm, like a thousand other masked faces. And it's profoundly soul transformative, this daily habit of asking the soul precisely what Jesus asks—"Why are you so afraid?"—because God knows what we've been slow to learn and slower to admit: Fear is about losing what we love.

Our deepest loves drive our deepest fears. "The evil in our desire typically does not lie in what we want, but that we want it too much" is what Calvin himself said.[1] Wherever one is afraid, one is afraid of losing what one loves. As Augustine pointed out, "We fear nothing save to lose what we love."[2] Jesus asks us to practice soul examine—to ask what we are so afraid of, so we can see what we love more than Him.

Ask your soul:

- What are you afraid of? What are you afraid might happen—or not happen? What are you afraid of for people you love? What are you afraid might happen in the future?
- How are your fears really about being startled at things that endanger beloved things—your hopes, your dreams, your relationships, your reputations, your futures, your senses of self?
- In what ways are you withdrawing from God—and what are you drawing closer to instead? What could possibly soothe your fears more than your Father Himself?
- What fears lurk behind your to-do lists, your hopes, all the things that seem to drive you? Take time, now, to pause and reflect.
- Where can you trace the hand of God and His gentle turning of your perspective, your attitude, your motivations, your heart posture this week? How do you see Him drawing you near?
- When you examine your own heart, what is the fear driving your heart toward sin? What if you examined your heart right now—and asked your Father to create in you a clean heart?
- As you make it a daily practice to examine your own heart, what would you do today if you had no fear?

The thing is: *Brave* doesn't mean feeling no fear. *Brave* simply means something—some*one*—is *more important* than feeling those fears.

As you ask yourself what Jesus asks His followers—"Why are you so afraid?" (Mark 4:40 NIV)—listen to the Way Himself speaking to you, a fresh revelation from His Word:

Fear nothing—not wild wolves in the night, not flying arrows in the day, not disease that prowls through the darkness, not disaster that erupts at high noon . . . because God's your refuge (Psalm 91:5–6, 9 MSG).

It is worthwhile to make it a daily rhythm to examine your soul when your head hits the pillow each night, asking that same question Jesus asks those following Him: "Why are you so afraid?" Because if you get into bed without cutting your fears down to size, you get into bed with the devil.

But: Unpack why you're afraid, and you send the devil packing.

Repeat these four words over and over and over, the prayer of your every heartbeat—*I trust You, Jesus*—and you invite Jesus to move right in and evict fear.

The sacred reality of this moment is: You don't stand alone, you don't walk alone, and you don't go alone. The words of 2 Timothy 4:17 give you a prayer to whisper to the parts of your heart that hold fear: "But the Lord stood at my side and gave me strength" (NIV). Nothing that can happen today or tomorrow or in the future will ever stop Him from sticking right there with you and giving you strength to do this hard thing, to walk this hard road. So there is nothing to fear—because there is nothing, no mess-up, no distraction, no less-than-hoped-for outcome, nothing in the universe that can happen today, to separate you from the loving hands of God. There is nothing to fear, no matter what—because *there is no sickness, no pain, no diagnosis, no death, nothing in the entire universe that can ever separate you from the loving hands of God.* He wrote your name right into His hand so He will never forget you. You are part of Him, and because of Christ going to the cross, you will never, ever have to fear a life apart from Him.

Since Jesus came to save us, there is no storm big enough to scare us, nothing ahead of us that's greater than the God behind us, and nothing that can go down and keep our God from holding us up.

Examine your heart's fears—and then examine how Jesus' heart of endless love for you washes over and washes away every single one of those fears. Still—and listen right now to your Abba Father's heart for you, *for you,* praying the Word over every one of your fears:

> The LORD himself goes before you and will be with you; he will never leave you nor forsake you. Do not be afraid; do not be discouraged (Deuteronomy 31:8 NIV).

When you know you are truly known and still fully loved, nothing can truly scare you. When you open up your hands and let go—you let all the fears go. When you live surrendered—you get to surrender all your fears. When you loosen your tight grip of control—you are cut loose from all your fears. When you live openhanded—you open the door to be freed from fear.

When we examine our own hearts is when our hearts can begin to experience real freedom. When you still and attend and examine your heart, know that Jesus stills everything to attend to your heart too. He examines the scars of your heart, tenderly transplants your heart, and gives you His own perfect, right, whole heart. The brokenness we find when we examine our hearts—the immeasurable grace for us in Jesus' heart is even greater.

You can cast out every fear today and you can leave behind every worry—because Jesus already crushed fear's head. He will never leave you, never forsake you, never stop carrying you. With God, *all things are possible!*

The One who went to the cross for you will let nothing cross your path that hasn't first crossed through His fingers of loving-kindness, which are over you. When you have a daily, sacred rhythm of examining the ways your heart turns—your very life can turn out far more fulfilling.

stillness to know God

How can I slow, still, and breathe in a place of trust with God today?
(Psalm 46:10)
Still all the worry.... Hush all the hurry.... Breathe ... breathe deeply....
I live in the spacious, non-anxious presence of God.

_____

attentiveness to hear God

Who do I say that God is today? (Mark 8:29)

_____

_____

_____

Where am I coming from and where am I going to today? (Genesis 16:8)

_____

_____

_____

What do I want today? (John 1:38)

_____

_____

_____

cruciformity to surrender to God

What do I need to do or surrender to live cruciform today? (Luke 9:23)

_____

_____

_____

revelation to see God

How did I experience a fresh revelation from God in His Word today? (Psalm 119:105)

_____

_____

_____

_____

_____

examine to return to God

What am I afraid of today? (Mark 4:40)

_____

_____

_____

_____

doxology to thank God

What can I thank God for today? (1 Thessalonians 5:18)

_____

_____

_____

What's God inviting me to do today, to make today a day of more amazing grace?

_____

_____

stillness to know God

How can I slow, still, and breathe in a place of trust with God today?
(Psalm 46:10)
Still all the worry. . . . Hush all the hurry. . . . Breathe . . . breathe deeply. . . .
I live in the spacious, non-anxious presence of God.

_____

attentiveness to hear God

Who do I say that God is today? (Mark 8:29)

_____

_____

_____

Where am I coming from and where am I going to today? (Genesis 16:8)

_____

_____

_____

What do I want today? (John 1:38)

_____

_____

_____

cruciformity to surrender to God

What do I need to do or surrender to live cruciform today? (Luke 9:23)

_____

_____

_____

revelation to see God

How did I experience a fresh revelation from God in His Word today?
(Psalm 119:105)

_____

_____

_____

_____

_____

examine to return to God

What am I afraid of today? (Mark 4:40)

_____

_____

_____

_____

doxology to thank God

What can I thank God for today? (1 Thessalonians 5:18)

_____

_____

_____

What's God inviting me to do today, to make today a day of more
amazing grace?

_____

_____

stillness to know God

How can I slow, still, and breathe in a place of trust with God today?
(Psalm 46:10)
Still all the worry.... Hush all the hurry.... Breathe ... breathe deeply....
I live in the spacious, non-anxious presence of God.

_____

attentiveness to hear God

Who do I say that God is today? (Mark 8:29)

_____

_____

_____

Where am I coming from and where am I going to today? (Genesis 16:8)

_____

_____

_____

What do I want today? (John 1:38)

_____

_____

_____

cruciformity to surrender to God

What do I need to do or surrender to live cruciform today? (Luke 9:23)

_____

_____

_____

revelation to see God

How did I experience a fresh revelation from God in His Word today?
(Psalm 119:105)

_____

_____

_____

_____

_____

examine to return to God

What am I afraid of today? (Mark 4:40)

_____

_____

_____

_____

doxology to thank God

What can I thank God for today? (1 Thessalonians 5:18)

_____

_____

_____

What's God inviting me to do today, to make today a day of more
amazing grace?

_____

_____

stillness to know God

How can I slow, still, and breathe in a place of trust with God today? (Psalm 46:10)
Still all the worry.... Hush all the hurry.... Breathe ... breathe deeply....
I live in the spacious, non-anxious presence of God.

_____

attentiveness to hear God

Who do I say that God is today? (Mark 8:29)

_____

_____

_____

Where am I coming from and where am I going to today? (Genesis 16:8)

_____

_____

_____

What do I want today? (John 1:38)

_____

_____

_____

cruciformity to surrender to God

What do I need to do or surrender to live cruciform today? (Luke 9:23)

_____

_____

_____

revelation to see God

How did I experience a fresh revelation from God in His Word today? (Psalm 119:105)

_____

_____

_____

_____

_____

examine to return to God

What am I afraid of today? (Mark 4:40)

_____

_____

_____

_____

doxology to thank God

What can I thank God for today? (1 Thessalonians 5:18)

_____

_____

_____

What's God inviting me to do today, to make today a day of more amazing grace?

_____

_____

stillness to know God

How can I slow, still, and breathe in a place of trust with God today?
(Psalm 46:10)
Still all the worry. . . . Hush all the hurry. . . . Breathe . . . breathe deeply. . . .
I live in the spacious, non-anxious presence of God.

_____

attentiveness to hear God

Who do I say that God is today? (Mark 8:29)

_____

_____

_____

Where am I coming from and where am I going to today? (Genesis 16:8)

_____

_____

_____

What do I want today? (John 1:38)

_____

_____

_____

cruciformity to surrender to God

What do I need to do or surrender to live cruciform today? (Luke 9:23)

_____

_____

_____

revelation to see God

How did I experience a fresh revelation from God in His Word today? (Psalm 119:105)

_____

_____

_____

_____

_____

examine to return to God

What am I afraid of today? (Mark 4:40)

_____

_____

_____

_____

doxology to thank God

What can I thank God for today? (1 Thessalonians 5:18)

_____

_____

_____

What's God inviting me to do today, to make today a day of more amazing grace?

_____

_____

stillness to know God

How can I slow, still, and breathe in a place of trust with God today?
(Psalm 46:10)
Still all the worry.... Hush all the hurry.... Breathe ... breathe deeply....
I live in the spacious, non-anxious presence of God.

_____

attentiveness to hear God

Who do I say that God is today? (Mark 8:29)

_____

_____

_____

Where am I coming from and where am I going to today? (Genesis 16:8)

_____

_____

_____

What do I want today? (John 1:38)

_____

_____

_____

cruciformity to surrender to God

What do I need to do or surrender to live cruciform today? (Luke 9:23)

_____

_____

_____

revelation to see God

How did I experience a fresh revelation from God in His Word today? (Psalm 119:105)

_____

_____

_____

_____

_____

examine to return to God

What am I afraid of today? (Mark 4:40)

_____

_____

_____

_____

_____

doxology to thank God

What can I thank God for today? (1 Thessalonians 5:18)

_____

_____

_____

What's God inviting me to do today, to make today a day of more amazing grace?

_____

_____

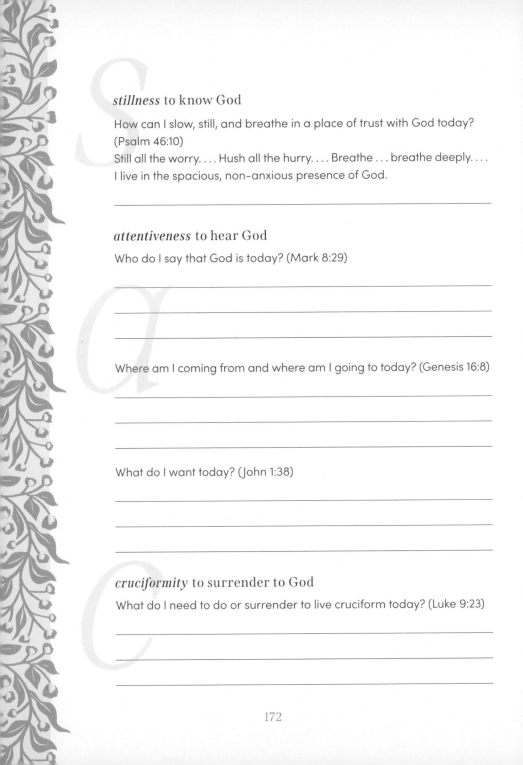

stillness to know God

How can I slow, still, and breathe in a place of trust with God today? (Psalm 46:10)
Still all the worry. . . . Hush all the hurry. . . . Breathe . . . breathe deeply. . . .
I live in the spacious, non-anxious presence of God.

_____

attentiveness to hear God

Who do I say that God is today? (Mark 8:29)

_____

_____

_____

Where am I coming from and where am I going to today? (Genesis 16:8)

_____

_____

_____

What do I want today? (John 1:38)

_____

_____

_____

cruciformity to surrender to God

What do I need to do or surrender to live cruciform today? (Luke 9:23)

_____

_____

_____

revelation to see God

How did I experience a fresh revelation from God in His Word today?
(Psalm 119:105)

_____

_____

_____

_____

_____

examine to return to God

What am I afraid of today? (Mark 4:40)

_____

_____

_____

_____

_____

doxology to thank God

What can I thank God for today? (1 Thessalonians 5:18)

_____

_____

_____

What's God inviting me to do today, to make today a day of more
amazing grace?

_____

_____

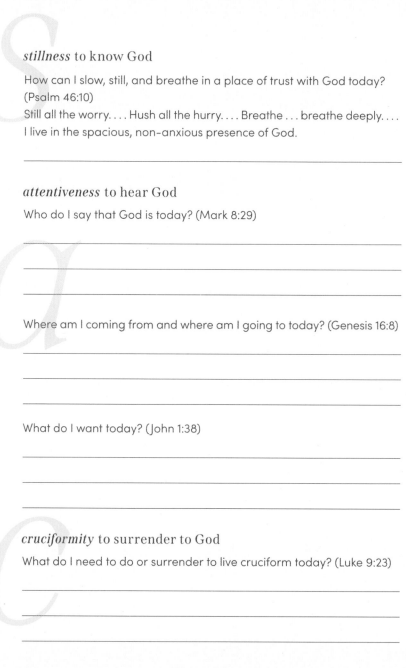

stillness to know God

How can I slow, still, and breathe in a place of trust with God today? (Psalm 46:10)

Still all the worry. . . . Hush all the hurry. . . . Breathe . . . breathe deeply. . . . I live in the spacious, non-anxious presence of God.

_____

attentiveness to hear God

Who do I say that God is today? (Mark 8:29)

_____

_____

_____

Where am I coming from and where am I going to today? (Genesis 16:8)

_____

_____

_____

What do I want today? (John 1:38)

_____

_____

_____

cruciformity to surrender to God

What do I need to do or surrender to live cruciform today? (Luke 9:23)

_____

_____

_____

revelation to see God

How did I experience a fresh revelation from God in His Word today?
(Psalm 119:105)

_____

_____

_____

_____

_____

examine to return to God

What am I afraid of today? (Mark 4:40)

_____

_____

_____

_____

_____

doxology to thank God

What can I thank God for today? (1 Thessalonians 5:18)

_____

_____

_____

What's God inviting me to do today, to make today a day of more
amazing grace?

_____

_____

stillness to know God

How can I slow, still, and breathe in a place of trust with God today?
(Psalm 46:10)
Still all the worry. . . . Hush all the hurry. . . . Breathe . . . breathe deeply. . . .
I live in the spacious, non-anxious presence of God.

---

attentiveness to hear God

Who do I say that God is today? (Mark 8:29)

Where am I coming from and where am I going to today? (Genesis 16:8)

What do I want today? (John 1:38)

---

cruciformity to surrender to God

What do I need to do or surrender to live cruciform today? (Luke 9:23)

---

revelation to see God

How did I experience a fresh revelation from God in His Word today?
(Psalm 119:105)

_____

_____

_____

_____

_____

examine to return to God

What am I afraid of today? (Mark 4:40)

_____

_____

_____

_____

doxology to thank God

What can I thank God for today? (1 Thessalonians 5:18)

_____

_____

_____

What's God inviting me to do today, to make today a day of more
amazing grace?

_____

_____

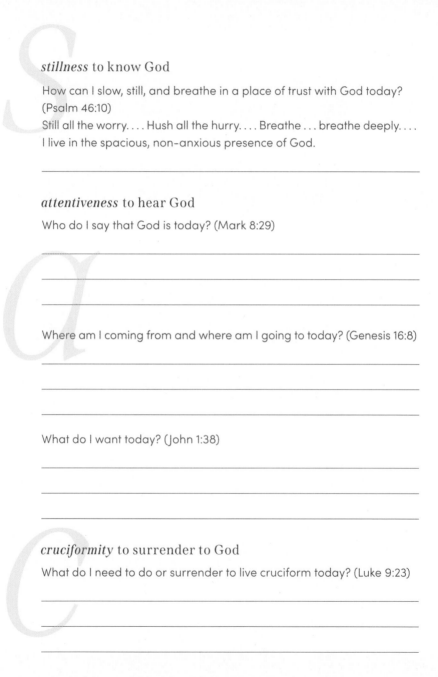

stillness to know God

How can I slow, still, and breathe in a place of trust with God today?
(Psalm 46:10)
Still all the worry.... Hush all the hurry.... Breathe ... breathe deeply....
I live in the spacious, non-anxious presence of God.

_____

attentiveness to hear God

Who do I say that God is today? (Mark 8:29)

_____

_____

_____

Where am I coming from and where am I going to today? (Genesis 16:8)

_____

_____

_____

What do I want today? (John 1:38)

_____

_____

_____

cruciformity to surrender to God

What do I need to do or surrender to live cruciform today? (Luke 9:23)

_____

_____

_____

revelation to see God

How did I experience a fresh revelation from God in His Word today?
(Psalm 119:105)

_____

_____

_____

_____

_____

examine to return to God

What am I afraid of today? (Mark 4:40)

_____

_____

_____

_____

_____

doxology to thank God

What can I thank God for today? (1 Thessalonians 5:18)

_____

_____

What's God inviting me to do today, to make today a day of more
amazing grace?

_____

_____

stillness to know God

How can I slow, still, and breathe in a place of trust with God today?
(Psalm 46:10)
Still all the worry. . . . Hush all the hurry. . . . Breathe . . . breathe deeply. . . .
I live in the spacious, non-anxious presence of God.

_____

attentiveness to hear God

Who do I say that God is today? (Mark 8:29)

_____

_____

_____

Where am I coming from and where am I going to today? (Genesis 16:8)

_____

_____

_____

What do I want today? (John 1:38)

_____

_____

_____

cruciformity to surrender to God

What do I need to do or surrender to live cruciform today? (Luke 9:23)

_____

_____

_____

revelation to see God

How did I experience a fresh revelation from God in His Word today? (Psalm 119:105)

_____

_____

_____

_____

_____

examine to return to God

What am I afraid of today? (Mark 4:40)

_____

_____

_____

_____

_____

doxology to thank God

What can I thank God for today? (1 Thessalonians 5:18)

_____

_____

_____

What's God inviting me to do today, to make today a day of more amazing grace?

_____

_____

stillness to know God

How can I slow, still, and breathe in a place of trust with God today? (Psalm 46:10)
Still all the worry.... Hush all the hurry.... Breathe ... breathe deeply....
I live in the spacious, non-anxious presence of God.

_____

attentiveness to hear God

Who do I say that God is today? (Mark 8:29)

_____

_____

_____

Where am I coming from and where am I going to today? (Genesis 16:8)

_____

_____

_____

What do I want today? (John 1:38)

_____

_____

_____

cruciformity to surrender to God

What do I need to do or surrender to live cruciform today? (Luke 9:23)

_____

_____

_____

revelation to see God

How did I experience a fresh revelation from God in His Word today?
(Psalm 119:105)

_____

_____

_____

_____

_____

examine to return to God

What am I afraid of today? (Mark 4:40)

_____

_____

_____

_____

_____

doxology to thank God

What can I thank God for today? (1 Thessalonians 5:18)

_____

_____

_____

What's God inviting me to do today, to make today a day of more
amazing grace?

_____

_____

stillness to know God

How can I slow, still, and breathe in a place of trust with God today?
(Psalm 46:10)
Still all the worry.... Hush all the hurry.... Breathe ... breathe deeply....
I live in the spacious, non-anxious presence of God.

_____

attentiveness to hear God

Who do I say that God is today? (Mark 8:29)

_____

_____

_____

Where am I coming from and where am I going to today? (Genesis 16:8)

_____

_____

_____

What do I want today? (John 1:38)

_____

_____

_____

cruciformity to surrender to God

What do I need to do or surrender to live cruciform today? (Luke 9:23)

_____

_____

_____

revelation to see God

How did I experience a fresh revelation from God in His Word today?
(Psalm 119:105)

_____

_____

_____

_____

_____

examine to return to God

What am I afraid of today? (Mark 4:40)

_____

_____

_____

_____

doxology to thank God

What can I thank God for today? (1 Thessalonians 5:18)

_____

_____

_____

What's God inviting me to do today, to make today a day of more
amazing grace?

_____

_____

stillness to know God

How can I slow, still, and breathe in a place of trust with God today?
(Psalm 46:10)
Still all the worry.... Hush all the hurry.... Breathe ... breathe deeply....
I live in the spacious, non-anxious presence of God.

_____

attentiveness to hear God

Who do I say that God is today? (Mark 8:29)

_____

_____

_____

Where am I coming from and where am I going to today? (Genesis 16:8)

_____

_____

_____

What do I want today? (John 1:38)

_____

_____

_____

cruciformity to surrender to God

What do I need to do or surrender to live cruciform today? (Luke 9:23)

_____

_____

_____

revelation to see God

How did I experience a fresh revelation from God in His Word today?
(Psalm 119:105)

_____

_____

_____

_____

_____

examine to return to God

What am I afraid of today? (Mark 4:40)

_____

_____

_____

_____

doxology to thank God

What can I thank God for today? (1 Thessalonians 5:18)

_____

_____

_____

What's God inviting me to do today, to make today a day of more
amazing grace?

_____

_____

stillness to know God

How can I slow, still, and breathe in a place of trust with God today? (Psalm 46:10)
Still all the worry.... Hush all the hurry.... Breathe ... breathe deeply.... I live in the spacious, non-anxious presence of God.

_____

attentiveness to hear God

Who do I say that God is today? (Mark 8:29)

_____

_____

_____

Where am I coming from and where am I going to today? (Genesis 16:8)

_____

_____

_____

What do I want today? (John 1:38)

_____

_____

_____

cruciformity to surrender to God

What do I need to do or surrender to live cruciform today? (Luke 9:23)

_____

_____

_____

revelation to see God

How did I experience a fresh revelation from God in His Word today?
(Psalm 119:105)

_____

_____

_____

_____

_____

examine to return to God

What am I afraid of today? (Mark 4:40)

_____

_____

_____

_____

_____

doxology to thank God

What can I thank God for today? (1 Thessalonians 5:18)

_____

_____

_____

What's God inviting me to do today, to make today a day of more
amazing grace?

_____

_____

Doxology

Why is it that we are always looking for sacred signs and answers instead of being so in love with Jesus we'd simply rather look with overwhelming gratitude into His sacred face?

Why is it that we always want to *know*? Tell us what will happen and when it will happen. *Give us the sacred sign, the answers, the promises we are looking for.* Give us some sign that we will know things are going to change, tell us what signs to look for, to know what is coming. Tell us the road ahead. Show us the way. Answer our prayers. Tell us what's going to happen in the end. The thing is, not knowing what is going to happen in the end is actually how we start to trust *now.*

In the middle of all our stories and heartbreak and unknowns, God knows that knowing your future won't enlarge your soul the way loving someone enough to trust them with your future will. Knowing *how* your future unfolds doesn't comfort you in the way trusting God *with* your future and letting Him enfold you in His arms *now* does.

Wherever you are, this is not the end. This is not the end of any heartbreak story, this is not the end of what seems impossible, this is not the end of your road, the end of your hopes, the end of your prayers.

You are not at the end of your story; you are only in the middle. And faith gives thanks in the middle of the story. Wherever you are right now:

Faith gives thanks in the middle of the story.
Faith gives thanks for this moment in the middle of the story.
Faith gives thanks for this detour in the middle of the story.
Faith gives thanks for this bend in the road in the middle of the story.

Faith sees how there is much to give thanks for now—which gives much hope and deepens much trust for the future, because the same loving God, who is giving grace upon grace now, will faithfully come with grace upon grace in the future too.

The truth is: You will discover the strength to live through today's crisis, and tomorrow's crisis, and every crisis coming—because just as *you can build a memory muscle as you exercise, you can build a gratitude muscle that builds a strong trust in God.*

Developing a muscle memory when you exercise means you've worked and practiced a motion so often that your body "remembers" what to do, how to move. So it too is possible to faithfully strengthen your gratitude muscle, so your soul remembers what to do in crisis: Do doxology. Give thanks. Build a strong trust in God, who will always provide more than enough grace for the challenges of every single day.

When you daily work out your gratitude doxology muscle, your soul remembers, even in crisis, how to keep turned toward God and His heart of love for you.

When you flex your doxology muscle day in and day out, your soul remembers what to do in heartbreak. The most important way to prepare for suffering is to be prepared to give thanks. Because even when we don't know what is coming up ahead, we prepare to keep turning to God, coming to God in thanks, because we trust, with all our hearts, that He still calls us beloved, that He still loves us with all His heart. We may not know what tomorrow holds, or what the road ahead of us holds—but when Jesus is our road, we know our road will hold and that Jesus holds us. How can we not give thanks?

Every time we *remember* to give thanks—God remembers all our broken places and gives us true joy, as we give Him true thanks.

The bottom-line truth is: We don't wait till we're joyful to be grateful, since being grateful . . . *is what makes us joyful.*

Gratitude isn't merely the way we feel some of the time; gratitude is the way we frame all of our lives. Thankfulness is more than a wave of emotion; it's a posture for our living.

The SACRED rhythm of every day must always end in doxology, because doxology literally saves us from the dark—because it gives us eyes to see how the grace of God, the gifts of God, is literally saving us every sacred moment.

Doxology or darkness—we always get to choose.

Ultimately, in his essence, Satan is an ingrate who chose ingratitude. Satan's rebellion led to the first sin of all humanity: *the sin of ingratitude*. Adam and Eve were, simply, painfully ungrateful for what God gave. Isn't that the catalyst for many of our sins? Our fall is—has always been and always will be—that we aren't satisfied in God and what He gives, but we hunger for something more, something other.

"The only real fall of man is his noneucharistic life, in a noneucharistic world."[1] That was the fall: Non-*eucharisteo*, ingratitude, was the fall—humanity's discontent with all that God freely gives. How in the world, for the sake of our joy, do we learn to live *eucharisteo*, to live eucharistically, a life of doxology? To count gifts and overcome the self-destructive habit of ingratitude with the saving habit of gratitude that leads us back to deep God-communion?

On the night Jesus was betrayed, when He was about to hold all the wrong, all the injustice, all the loss, grief, sin, and every last bit of all the broken and busted the world has ever known—what did Jesus do?

"He took bread, gave thanks and broke it, and gave it to them" (Luke 22:19).

In the original language "He gave thanks" reads *eucharisteo*. The root word of *eucharisteo* is *charis*, meaning grace.

Jesus took the bread and saw it as grace and gave thanks. He took the bread and knew it to be a gift and gave thanks. But there is more: While *eucharisteo*, thanksgiving, holds the Greek word for grace, *charis*, it also holds its derivative, the Greek word *chara*, meaning joy. *Joy.* Deep *chara*-joy is found only at the table of thanksgiving.

Charis. Grace. *Eucharisteo.* Thanksgiving. *Chara*. Joy.

A triplet of stars, a constellation in the black. A threefold cord that might hold a life. Offer a way into the fullest life. Grace, thanksgiving, joy. Eucharisteo. *A Greek word that makes meaning of everything.*

If Jesus, on the night He was betrayed, chose to give thanks for the cup of suffering because—out of a cosmos of possibilities—thanksgiving was the preferred weapon to face and fight the dark, do we have any better choice when we feel betrayed by hope and people and God? And if Jesus can give thanks even on the night He was brutally betrayed, what if we practiced giving thanks in the midst of our feeling betrayed by God?

A habit of thankfulness is always our exodus from bitterness.

Here, in this SACRED moment, it is all true for you: "He who did not spare his own Son, but gave him up for us all—how will he not also, along with him, graciously give us all things?" (Romans 8:32 NIV). He gave us Jesus. Jesus! *Gave Him up for us all.* He washed our grime with the bloody grace. He drove the iron ore through His own vein. If God didn't withhold from us His very own Son, will God withhold anything we need? If trust must be earned, hasn't God unequivocally earned our trust with the bark on the raw wounds, the thorns pressed into the brow, your name on the cracked lips?

How will He not also graciously give us all things He deems best and right? He's already given the incomprehensible: Himself. How will He not also give us all we ever need—since He already gave us everything that He is? If Jesus stretched open His arms to offer you all of Himself, is there anything you need that He also won't freely give you? How can you not then "give thanks in all circumstances; for this is God's will for you in Christ Jesus" (1 Thessalonians 5:18 NIV), "always giving thanks to God the Father for everything, in the name of our Lord Jesus Christ" (Ephesians 5:20 NIV)?

When there's this daily sacred rhythm of putting pen to paper as a prayer of thankfulness, all of life becomes a song of doxology:

For beaded necklaces of dew slipping down branches of the spruce tree every morning . . .

For steam rising from the kettle like everyday incense . . .

For a beloved voice on the other end of the connection, connecting their heart to yours in a world of aloneness . . .

For mourning doves crooning at the window . . .

For an east breeze dancing with the light in the trees . . .

For God's Word beckoning, calling, speaking, comforting, strengthening, remaking, restoring, and re-storying . . .

For breath in the lungs, and the gift of this heartbeat, and this sacred moment here . . .

Count the gifts, and you genuinely begin to see who you can always count on to sustain you with His all-sufficient grace. And unless you count even the hard things as holy gifts, you've miscounted the gifts and misunderstood His heart and ways He works all things together for good. It may be easier to give God thanks for all that looks like bouquets of goodness in your life—but the fullest life unfurls when you trust God deeply enough to give Him thanks even for the thorns. To give Him thanks exactly when it's the hardest to. Because thankfulness for thorns produces a kind of faithfulness that has roots in His goodness no matter what, and *that kind of faith produces more than blooms*—it produces real fruit that lasts for all eternity. It's the thorns in your life that can root you in what ultimately really matters in your life.

Because in the most tender of stories, it turns out: You can be thankful for the thorns in your life when you let them pierce your heart right to Jesus' heart.

You can be thankful for the thorns—when you let them drive you deeper into the comfort of Christ.

You can be thankful for the thorns, when you let the thorn in your side affix you to the pierced side of Jesus—and shape and form you more like Jesus Himself.

It's the thorns of life that make the comfort of Christ your everything.

It turns out? The secret, sacred way to joy is to keep practicing giving thanks *exactly when you don't want to.*

The Lamb of God wore a crown of thorns for you—how can we not give Him thanks for our thorns that press us into Him?

Doxology, doxology, doxology.

In the end, no matter what the road has held or where the road has led, the Way Himself will carry you all the way home, and when you arrive at the sacred chambers of His presence, this will be all there is, this holy joy:

Enter with the password: "Thank you!"
Make yourselves at home, talking praise.
Thank him. Worship him.
For GOD is sheer beauty,
all-generous in love,
loyal always and ever" (Psalm 100:4–5 MSG).

Gratitude gets us home to God.

A sacred life is always a eucharistic life; a meaningful life is always a thankful life. And any way of life that finds a way through has always had the sacred cadence of doxology.

Doxology, doxology, doxology.

The Doxology

Praise God from whom all blessings flow;

Praise Him all creatures here below;

Praise Him above, ye heav'nly host;

Praise Father, Son, and Holy Ghost.

stillness to know God

How can I slow, still, and breathe in a place of trust with God today?
(Psalm 46:10)
Still all the worry.... Hush all the hurry.... Breathe ... breathe deeply....
I live in the spacious, non-anxious presence of God.

_____

attentiveness to hear God

Who do I say that God is today? (Mark 8:29)

_____

_____

_____

Where am I coming from and where am I going to today? (Genesis 16:8)

_____

_____

_____

What do I want today? (John 1:38)

_____

_____

_____

cruciformity to surrender to God

What do I need to do or surrender to live cruciform today? (Luke 9:23)

_____

_____

_____

revelation to see God

How did I experience a fresh revelation from God in His Word today?
(Psalm 119:105)

_____

_____

_____

_____

_____

examine to return to God

What am I afraid of today? (Mark 4:40)

_____

_____

_____

_____

_____

doxology to thank God

What can I thank God for today? (1 Thessalonians 5:18)

_____

_____

_____

What's God inviting me to do today, to make today a day of more
amazing grace?

_____

_____

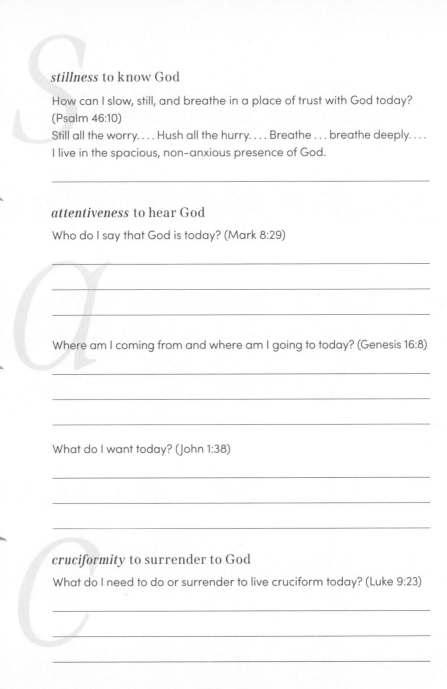

stillness to know God

How can I slow, still, and breathe in a place of trust with God today?
(Psalm 46:10)
Still all the worry.... Hush all the hurry.... Breathe ... breathe deeply....
I live in the spacious, non-anxious presence of God.

_____

attentiveness to hear God

Who do I say that God is today? (Mark 8:29)

_____

_____

_____

Where am I coming from and where am I going to today? (Genesis 16:8)

_____

_____

_____

What do I want today? (John 1:38)

_____

_____

_____

cruciformity to surrender to God

What do I need to do or surrender to live cruciform today? (Luke 9:23)

_____

_____

_____

revelation to see God

How did I experience a fresh revelation from God in His Word today? (Psalm 119:105)

_____

_____

_____

_____

_____

examine to return to God

What am I afraid of today? (Mark 4:40)

_____

_____

_____

_____

_____

doxology to thank God

What can I thank God for today? (1 Thessalonians 5:18)

_____

_____

What's God inviting me to do today, to make today a day of more amazing grace?

_____

_____

stillness to know God

How can I slow, still, and breathe in a place of trust with God today? (Psalm 46:10)
Still all the worry.... Hush all the hurry.... Breathe ... breathe deeply....
I live in the spacious, non-anxious presence of God.

_____

attentiveness to hear God

Who do I say that God is today? (Mark 8:29)

_____

_____

_____

Where am I coming from and where am I going to today? (Genesis 16:8)

_____

_____

_____

What do I want today? (John 1:38)

_____

_____

_____

cruciformity to surrender to God

What do I need to do or surrender to live cruciform today? (Luke 9:23)

_____

_____

_____

revelation to see God

How did I experience a fresh revelation from God in His Word today?
(Psalm 119:105)

_____

_____

_____

_____

_____

examine to return to God

What am I afraid of today? (Mark 4:40)

_____

_____

_____

_____

doxology to thank God

What can I thank God for today? (1 Thessalonians 5:18)

_____

_____

_____

What's God inviting me to do today, to make today a day of more
amazing grace?

_____

_____

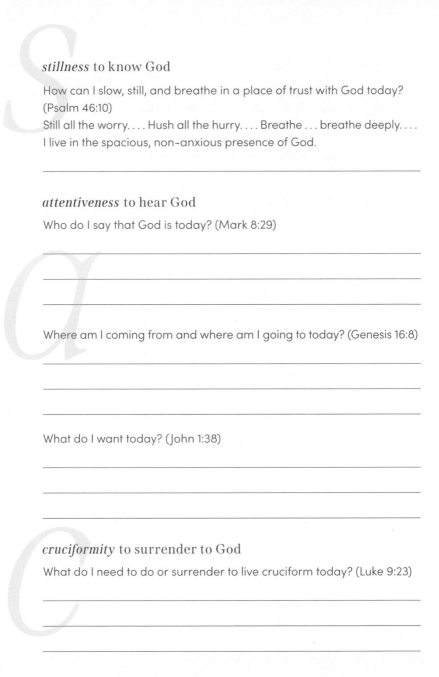

stillness to know God

How can I slow, still, and breathe in a place of trust with God today?
(Psalm 46:10)
Still all the worry.... Hush all the hurry.... Breathe ... breathe deeply....
I live in the spacious, non-anxious presence of God.

_____

attentiveness to hear God

Who do I say that God is today? (Mark 8:29)

_____

_____

_____

Where am I coming from and where am I going to today? (Genesis 16:8)

_____

_____

_____

What do I want today? (John 1:38)

_____

_____

_____

cruciformity to surrender to God

What do I need to do or surrender to live cruciform today? (Luke 9:23)

_____

_____

_____

revelation to see God

How did I experience a fresh revelation from God in His Word today?
(Psalm 119:105)

_____

_____

_____

_____

_____

examine to return to God

What am I afraid of today? (Mark 4:40)

_____

_____

_____

_____

_____

doxology to thank God

What can I thank God for today? (1 Thessalonians 5:18)

_____

_____

_____

What's God inviting me to do today, to make today a day of more
amazing grace?

_____

_____

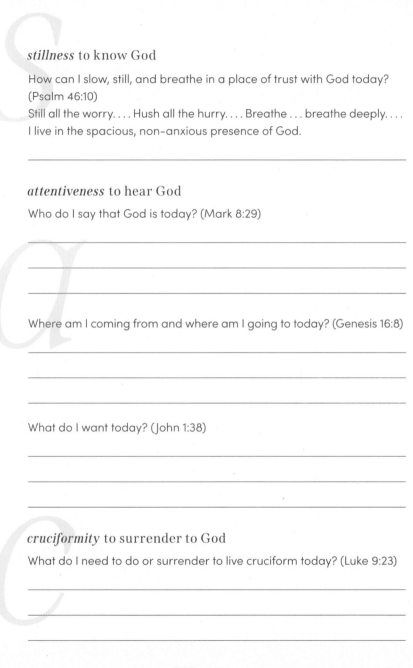

stillness to know God

How can I slow, still, and breathe in a place of trust with God today? (Psalm 46:10)

Still all the worry. . . . Hush all the hurry. . . . Breathe . . . breathe deeply. . . . I live in the spacious, non-anxious presence of God.

_____

attentiveness to hear God

Who do I say that God is today? (Mark 8:29)

_____

_____

_____

Where am I coming from and where am I going to today? (Genesis 16:8)

_____

_____

_____

What do I want today? (John 1:38)

_____

_____

_____

cruciformity to surrender to God

What do I need to do or surrender to live cruciform today? (Luke 9:23)

_____

_____

_____

revelation to see God

How did I experience a fresh revelation from God in His Word today? (Psalm 119:105)

_____

_____

_____

_____

_____

examine to return to God

What am I afraid of today? (Mark 4:40)

_____

_____

_____

_____

_____

doxology to thank God

What can I thank God for today? (1 Thessalonians 5:18)

_____

_____

_____

What's God inviting me to do today, to make today a day of more amazing grace?

_____

_____

stillness to know God

How can I slow, still, and breathe in a place of trust with God today? (Psalm 46:10)
Still all the worry. . . . Hush all the hurry. . . . Breathe . . . breathe deeply. . . .
I live in the spacious, non-anxious presence of God.

_____

attentiveness to hear God

Who do I say that God is today? (Mark 8:29)

_____

_____

_____

Where am I coming from and where am I going to today? (Genesis 16:8)

_____

_____

_____

What do I want today? (John 1:38)

_____

_____

_____

cruciformity to surrender to God

What do I need to do or surrender to live cruciform today? (Luke 9:23)

_____

_____

_____

revelation to see God

How did I experience a fresh revelation from God in His Word today?
(Psalm 119:105)

_____

_____

_____

_____

_____

examine to return to God

What am I afraid of today? (Mark 4:40)

_____

_____

_____

_____

doxology to thank God

What can I thank God for today? (1 Thessalonians 5:18)

_____

_____

_____

What's God inviting me to do today, to make today a day of more
amazing grace?

_____

_____

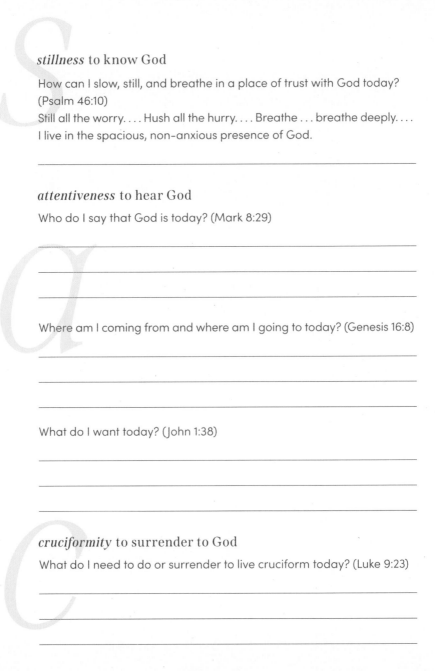

stillness to know God

How can I slow, still, and breathe in a place of trust with God today?
(Psalm 46:10)
Still all the worry. . . . Hush all the hurry. . . . Breathe . . . breathe deeply. . . .
I live in the spacious, non-anxious presence of God.

_____

attentiveness to hear God

Who do I say that God is today? (Mark 8:29)

_____

_____

_____

Where am I coming from and where am I going to today? (Genesis 16:8)

_____

_____

_____

What do I want today? (John 1:38)

_____

_____

_____

cruciformity to surrender to God

What do I need to do or surrender to live cruciform today? (Luke 9:23)

_____

_____

revelation to see God

How did I experience a fresh revelation from God in His Word today?
(Psalm 119:105)

_____

_____

_____

_____

_____

examine to return to God

What am I afraid of today? (Mark 4:40)

_____

_____

_____

_____

_____

doxology to thank God

What can I thank God for today? (1 Thessalonians 5:18)

_____

_____

_____

What's God inviting me to do today, to make today a day of more
amazing grace?

_____

_____

stillness to know God

How can I slow, still, and breathe in a place of trust with God today? (Psalm 46:10)
Still all the worry. . . . Hush all the hurry. . . . Breathe . . . breathe deeply. . . .
I live in the spacious, non-anxious presence of God.

_____

attentiveness to hear God

Who do I say that God is today? (Mark 8:29)

_____

_____

_____

Where am I coming from and where am I going to today? (Genesis 16:8)

_____

_____

_____

What do I want today? (John 1:38)

_____

_____

_____

cruciformity to surrender to God

What do I need to do or surrender to live cruciform today? (Luke 9:23)

_____

_____

_____

revelation to see God

How did I experience a fresh revelation from God in His Word today? (Psalm 119:105)

_____

_____

_____

_____

_____

examine to return to God

What am I afraid of today? (Mark 4:40)

_____

_____

_____

_____

doxology to thank God

What can I thank God for today? (1 Thessalonians 5:18)

_____

_____

What's God inviting me to do today, to make today a day of more amazing grace?

_____

_____

stillness to know God

How can I slow, still, and breathe in a place of trust with God today?
(Psalm 46:10)
Still all the worry. . . . Hush all the hurry. . . . Breathe . . . breathe deeply. . . .
I live in the spacious, non-anxious presence of God.

_____

attentiveness to hear God

Who do I say that God is today? (Mark 8:29)

_____

_____

_____

Where am I coming from and where am I going to today? (Genesis 16:8)

_____

_____

_____

What do I want today? (John 1:38)

_____

_____

_____

cruciformity to surrender to God

What do I need to do or surrender to live cruciform today? (Luke 9:23)

_____

_____

_____

revelation to see God

How did I experience a fresh revelation from God in His Word today?
(Psalm 119:105)

_____

_____

_____

_____

_____

examine to return to God

What am I afraid of today? (Mark 4:40)

_____

_____

_____

_____

doxology to thank God

What can I thank God for today? (1 Thessalonians 5:18)

_____

_____

_____

What's God inviting me to do today, to make today a day of more
amazing grace?

_____

_____

stillness to know God

How can I slow, still, and breathe in a place of trust with God today?
(Psalm 46:10)
Still all the worry. . . . Hush all the hurry. . . . Breathe . . . breathe deeply. . . .
I live in the spacious, non-anxious presence of God.

_____

attentiveness to hear God

Who do I say that God is today? (Mark 8:29)

_____

_____

_____

Where am I coming from and where am I going to today? (Genesis 16:8)

_____

_____

_____

What do I want today? (John 1:38)

_____

_____

_____

cruciformity to surrender to God

What do I need to do or surrender to live cruciform today? (Luke 9:23)

_____

_____

_____

revelation to see God

How did I experience a fresh revelation from God in His Word today?
(Psalm 119:105)

_____

_____

_____

_____

_____

examine to return to God

What am I afraid of today? (Mark 4:40)

_____

_____

_____

_____

doxology to thank God

What can I thank God for today? (1 Thessalonians 5:18)

_____

_____

_____

What's God inviting me to do today, to make today a day of more
amazing grace?

_____

_____

stillness to know God

How can I slow, still, and breathe in a place of trust with God today?
(Psalm 46:10)
Still all the worry. . . . Hush all the hurry. . . . Breathe . . . breathe deeply. . . .
I live in the spacious, non-anxious presence of God.

_____

attentiveness to hear God

Who do I say that God is today? (Mark 8:29)

_____

_____

_____

Where am I coming from and where am I going to today? (Genesis 16:8)

_____

_____

_____

What do I want today? (John 1:38)

_____

_____

_____

cruciformity to surrender to God

What do I need to do or surrender to live cruciform today? (Luke 9:23)

_____

_____

_____

revelation to see God

How did I experience a fresh revelation from God in His Word today?
(Psalm 119:105)

_____

_____

_____

_____

_____

examine to return to God

What am I afraid of today? (Mark 4:40)

_____

_____

_____

_____

_____

doxology to thank God

What can I thank God for today? (1 Thessalonians 5:18)

_____

_____

_____

What's God inviting me to do today, to make today a day of more
amazing grace?

_____

_____

stillness to know God

How can I slow, still, and breathe in a place of trust with God today?
(Psalm 46:10)
Still all the worry. . . . Hush all the hurry. . . . Breathe . . . breathe deeply. . . .
I live in the spacious, non-anxious presence of God.

_____

attentiveness to hear God

Who do I say that God is today? (Mark 8:29)

_____

_____

_____

Where am I coming from and where am I going to today? (Genesis 16:8)

_____

_____

_____

What do I want today? (John 1:38)

_____

_____

_____

cruciformity to surrender to God

What do I need to do or surrender to live cruciform today? (Luke 9:23)

_____

_____

_____

revelation to see God

How did I experience a fresh revelation from God in His Word today? (Psalm 119:105)

_____

_____

_____

_____

_____

examine to return to God

What am I afraid of today? (Mark 4:40)

_____

_____

_____

_____

_____

doxology to thank God

What can I thank God for today? (1 Thessalonians 5:18)

_____

_____

_____

What's God inviting me to do today, to make today a day of more amazing grace?

_____

_____

stillness to know God

How can I slow, still, and breathe in a place of trust with God today?
(Psalm 46:10)
Still all the worry.... Hush all the hurry.... Breathe ... breathe deeply....
I live in the spacious, non-anxious presence of God.

_____

attentiveness to hear God

Who do I say that God is today? (Mark 8:29)

_____

_____

_____

Where am I coming from and where am I going to today? (Genesis 16:8)

_____

_____

_____

What do I want today? (John 1:38)

_____

_____

_____

cruciformity to surrender to God

What do I need to do or surrender to live cruciform today? (Luke 9:23)

_____

_____

_____

revelation to see God

How did I experience a fresh revelation from God in His Word today? (Psalm 119:105)

_____

_____

_____

_____

_____

examine to return to God

What am I afraid of today? (Mark 4:40)

_____

_____

_____

_____

_____

doxology to thank God

What can I thank God for today? (1 Thessalonians 5:18)

_____

_____

_____

What's God inviting me to do today, to make today a day of more amazing grace?

_____

_____

stillness to know God

How can I slow, still, and breathe in a place of trust with God today?
(Psalm 46:10)
Still all the worry. . . . Hush all the hurry. . . . Breathe . . . breathe deeply. . . .
I live in the spacious, non-anxious presence of God.

_____

attentiveness to hear God

Who do I say that God is today? (Mark 8:29)

_____

_____

_____

Where am I coming from and where am I going to today? (Genesis 16:8)

_____

_____

_____

What do I want today? (John 1:38)

_____

_____

_____

cruciformity to surrender to God

What do I need to do or surrender to live cruciform today? (Luke 9:23)

_____

_____

_____

revelation to see God

How did I experience a fresh revelation from God in His Word today?
(Psalm 119:105)

_____

_____

_____

_____

_____

examine to return to God

What am I afraid of today? (Mark 4:40)

_____

_____

_____

_____

_____

doxology to thank God

What can I thank God for today? (1 Thessalonians 5:18)

_____

_____

_____

What's God inviting me to do today, to make today a day of more
amazing grace?

_____

_____

stillness to know God

How can I slow, still, and breathe in a place of trust with God today?
(Psalm 46:10)
Still all the worry.... Hush all the hurry.... Breathe ... breathe deeply....
I live in the spacious, non-anxious presence of God.

_____

attentiveness to hear God

Who do I say that God is today? (Mark 8:29)

_____

_____

_____

Where am I coming from and where am I going to today? (Genesis 16:8)

_____

_____

_____

What do I want today? (John 1:38)

_____

_____

_____

cruciformity to surrender to God

What do I need to do or surrender to live cruciform today? (Luke 9:23)

_____

_____

_____

revelation to see God

How did I experience a fresh revelation from God in His Word today?
(Psalm 119:105)

_____

_____

_____

_____

_____

examine to return to God

What am I afraid of today? (Mark 4:40)

_____

_____

_____

_____

_____

doxology to thank God

What can I thank God for today? (1 Thessalonians 5:18)

_____

_____

_____

What's God inviting me to do today, to make today a day of more
amazing grace?

_____

_____

ABOUT THE AUTHOR

ANN VOSKAMP is the wife of a farmer, mama to seven, and the author of the *New York Times* bestsellers *The Broken Way, The Greatest Gift, Unwrapping the Greatest Gift,* and the sixty-week *New York Times* bestseller *One Thousand Gifts: A Dare to Live Fully Right Where You Are,* which has sold more than 1.5 million copies and has been translated into more than twenty languages. Named by *Christianity Today* as one of fifty women most shaping culture and the church today, Ann knows unspoken broken, big country skies, and an intimacy with God that touches tender places. Cofounder of ShowUpNow.com, Ann is a passionate advocate for the marginalized and oppressed around the globe, partnering with Mercy House Global, Compassion International, and artisans around the world through her fair-trade community, Grace Case. She and her husband took a leap of faith to restore a 125-year-old stone church into The Village Table—a place where everyone has a seat and belongs. Join the journey at www. annvoskamp.com or instagram/annvoskamp.

NOTES

Introduction

1. Brett Q. ford et al., "The Psychological Health Benefits of Accepting Negative Emotions and Thoughts: Laboratory, Diary, and Longitudinal Evidence," *Journal of Personality and Social Psychology* 155, no. 6 (2018): 1075–92, https://www.ncbi.nlm.nih.gov.
2. Lydia Denworth, "The Connection Between Writing and Sleep," *Psychology Today*, January 12, 2018, https://www.psychologytoday.com/us
3. Bridget Murray, "Writing to Heal," *Monitor on Psychology, American Psychological Association,* 33, no. 6 (June 2022), 54: https://www.apa.org.
4. Dr. Howard Taylor and Mrs. Howard Taylor, *Hudson Taylor and the China Inland Mission: The Growth of a Work of God* (London: Morgan & Scott, 1920), 201–2.
5. Taylor and Taylor, *Hudson Taylor and the China Inland Mission*, 213.
6. Ann Voskamp, *WayMaker: Finding the Way to the Life You've Always Dreamed Of* (Nashville: Thomas Nelson, 2022).
7. Jeremy Sutton PhD, "5 Benefits of Journaling for Mental Health," PositivePsychology.com, May 14, 2018, https://positivepsychology.com.

Stillness

1. F. B. Meyer, *Psalms: Bible Readings* (Eugene, OR: Wipf & Stock, 2016), 60.
2. NAS Exhaustive Concordance, s.v. "raphah," accessed February 21, 2024, https://biblehub.com.
3. Ole Hallesby, *Under His Wings* (Minneapolis: Augsburg, 1932), 13.

Attention

1. Curt Thompson, *The Soul of Shame: Retelling the Stories We Believe about Ourselves* (Downers Grove, IL: IVP Books, 2015), 124.
2. A. W. Tozer, *The Knowledge of the Holy: The Attributes of God. Their Meaning in the Christian Life* (Cambridge, UK: Lutterworth Press, 2022).
3. C. S. Lewis, *Letters of C. S. Lewis*, ed. W. H. Lewis (New York: Harcourt Brace & World, 1966), 407.

Cruciform

1. C. S. Lewis, *The Four Loves* (New York: Harcourt Brace, 1960), 121.

Revelation

1. Abraham Joshua Heschel, *The Prophets* (Peabody, MA: Hendrickson, 1962), 57.

Examine

1. John Calvin, *Institutes of the Christian Religion*, ed. John T. McNeill (Philadelphia: Westminster, 1960), 1.11.8.
2. Saint Augustine, *The Confessions of Saint Augustine*, trans. E. B. Pusey (Project Gutenberg, 2002), bk. 2, https://www.gutenberg.org/files/3296/3296-h/3296-h.htm.

Doxology

1. Alexander Schmemann, *For the Life of the World: Sacraments and Orthodoxy* (Crestwood, NY: St. Vladimir's Seminary Press, 2004), 18.

bba, Almighty God, Ancient of Days, C
ce, Eternal King, Everlasting Father, For
ce, Holy One, Hope, Just and Mighty One
ht, Lord of All the Earth, Maker of heave
rince of Peace, Protector, Refuge, Rock, I
ig Tower, Sustainer of my Soul, Upholder
oa, Almighty God, Ancient of Days, Cons
rnal King, Everlasting Father, Fortress, (
y One, Hope, Just and Mighty One, Keep
d of All the Earth, Maker of heaven and
f Peace, Protector, Refuge, Rock, Ruler of
er, Sustainer of my Soul, Upholder of My
ighty God, Ancient of Days, Consuming
g, Everlasting Father, Fortress, God of Al
e, Just and Mighty One, Keeper, King of
e Earth, Maker of heaven and earth, My